The Crucible of the Future

The Crucible of the Future

A Prophetic Look at the Nineties

Tribulations
Transitions and
Triumphs

A prophetic book on the last days

and restoration of the church.

God's strategy:
"A restored church with a restored gospel."

DALE RUMBLE

 Unless otherwise identified, Scripture quotations are from the New American Standard translation of the Bible.

Destiny Image Publishers
P.O. Box 351
Shippensburg, PA 17257

"Speaking to the Purposes of God for this Generation"

ISBN 0-914903-89-6

For Worldwide Distribution
Printed in the U.S.A.

Dedication

TO ALL MEMBERS OF THE
BODY OF CHRIST

Acknowledgments

I wish to express my thanks to Carl Kinbar, Donald Rumble and Don Nori for their review of the text.

I also thank my wife Bertha for her encouragement and prayers for me.

Contents

Foreword

What would motivate an Oklahoma minister to write the foreword for a book written by a New York author whom he never had met? The answer is found in the content of the book. Dale Rumble's, *The Crucible of the Future,* presents with clarity the vision which has become the heartbeat of Tulsa Christian Fellowship. As an elder of TCF, I am eager to expose this vision to the Church at large.

When I read the manuscript of Dale Rumble's, *The Crucible of the Future,* I felt much like the writer, who, upon his first reading of ancient literature, cried out, "Curse these ancients! They've stolen our best ideas!" Of course, my response to the manuscript was a joyous, "Praise God! Here is a brother, unknown to us, who has reached the same conclusions as we!" In this book, not only does Dale Rumble deliver a pure presentation of New Testament Church life, but he presents it as the prescription for what ails the Body of Christ.

Throughout the nation, perhaps even the world, there is a growing dissatisfaction with conditions in the church. There is a sense that something is wrong, especially in the area of church government.

The one-man pastor system, so popular in most

evangelical and charismatic churches, has produced a host of tragedies. In most cases, so much is demanded of one man that only the strongest and most gifted can handle the "job" without serious spiritual damage. In most situations, the "Pastor" has to produce more bodies and bucks each year or the church board will find a way to replace him. Those who succeed in this system, have to battle the temptation to pride. The number of pastors "leaving the ministry" each year because of this system is well known.

The clergy-laity dichotomy in the modern church has resulted in a professional view of ministry. As R. Paul Stevens has pointed out in his excellent book, *Liberating the Laity,* professionalism has stunted the Church. Professionalism is the assertion that certain activities can be performed only by a professional; and that any professional can perform those activities. Thus, professionals can be exchanged without any problem in the Church. This results in a church composed of spectators. The task Divinely given to the Church never can be accomplished with most of the members sitting in the bleachers watching the professionals perform.

Current hierarchical structures tempt the professionals to "ladder climbing." The desire for titles and position are far from the spirit of our Lord's teaching (Matthew 23:6-12).

What can be done? Some groups have tried to reform by attempting to correct current evils, but still retaining the system. Such reforms will result only in temporary correction. The systems themselves create the problems.

The only feasible answer is a radical restructuring of the Church. The only alternative worthy of consideration is the one given in the New Testament under the guidance of the Holy Spirit. From the time that the Church departed from this pattern, the flaws present in human nature began to characterize the Church.

Restoration, rather than reformation, is the cure. Dale Rumble presents the thesis that the Holy Spirit is orchestrating such a restoration as the Church moves toward the close of this century. Readers not acquainted with early church literature will find a helpful survey of that literature and resulting scholarly comments presented in the section entitled, "Historical Record of the First Church." It is this record that verifies the conclusions reached in New Testament study.

One final word — although this is a book of principles, it is not a book of untried theories. The patterns set forth already are being implemented successfully in a growing number of churches, both in the U.S. and abroad. Hopefully, the arrival of this book will increase that number.

James W. Garrett

Introduction

I have been impressed by the number of prophetic messages I have heard this year (1988) containing phrases such as the following, "this is a year of new beginnings for my people"; "events coming upon the earth will shake all that can be shaken"; "things will not continue to be in the future as they have in the past"; "behavior I have winked at among my people until now I will no longer tolerate", etc.

I personally have an intuitive sense that 1988 is the first year of a new era, perhaps the last generation of this church age. In any case, it appears that we are entering a time of new shakings, new testings, new challenges, new dimensions of spiritual warfare, but most of all a time of new manifestation of Lord's power, grace and glory upon the church. It is a time of restoration!

It is significant that 1988 was the first year of Jubilee since A.D. 27, the year that Jesus began His ministry. [1] A valid Jubilee can only take place with Israel in their land. In A.D. 76, the next date for a Jubilee, the temple had been destroyed and the Jews dispersed. Israel again became a nation in 1948 ten years after the Jubilee period of 1938/39. The first possible Jubilee, since the days of Jesus, began in October 1987.

This covers a time period of forty Jubilee periods (i.e., 49x40=1960+27=1987).

I suspect that when we look back in an historical sense we will discover that 1988 was indeed a year that marked the beginning of significant change and transition. The stage is being set for dramatic events that will ultimately climax in the Lord's return; He is building and restoring the church for that day.

We should not be overly engrossed with what takes place in the national, economic, political and social arenas. To do so would be to take our eyes off of the Lord. On the other hand, we had better give full attention to the spiritual significance of such happenings and to what God may be speaking to the church through them.

The United States is a country standing on the verge of God's judgement for sin, in particular, for the practices of abortion and homosexuality. In 1988, with a rising AIDS epidemic we have seen great destruction by forest fires in the west, a severe farm drought with the hottest summer temperature on record. And we can expect turmoil and tribulation to increase in the future. However, God's promise is that His glory will arise upon the church during days of deepening darkness in the world (Is. 60:1-2). Therefore, we need to tune our ears to hear what He is speaking today concerning the church.

When you speak of building a New Testament Church, or of God restoring the church, many leaders look askance at you. I like the way Arthur Wallis expresses it in his book, *The Radical Christian*: [2]

> To many, what has been written in this book regarding God's way for His Church will be dismissed as idealistic, impractical or superspiritual. They will tell us that institutionalized Christianity is too well established. A New Testament Church today is a pipe dream. No leader of any stature

> would entertain it. In a word, it can never be. Then let us remember God's word to Sarah when, in her unbelief, she too laughed off God's promise to her as an impossibility: *"Is anything too hard for the Lord?"* (p 161)

Most Christian books are written on what God has done in the past and on what we can learn from those visitations. There are also many books devoted to various needs, issues and problems confronting the church today as well as methodologies to address them. However, there is too little published on what the Lord is *currently* speaking to the church. By God's grace that is what I have attempted to do. Although I may not have done it well, my intent has been to express the heart of God for the church today.

In 1982, *The Diakonate* was written to address the servant qualities that the Lord requires in the lives of men who will lead the way in church restoration.

In 1986, *Prepared For His Glory* was a presentation of those foundation truths, as I understand them, that are necessary to build a New Testament church. The text was developed around graphic models of spirit, soul and body.

The Crucible of The Future builds upon the contents of the previous two books and addresses the significance of where we are timewise in church restoration. Important transitions are pointed out that leaders will face in the areas of their commitment to the Lord's strategy for these days.

The historical record of the early church's falling away over the first two centuries is examined to understand how the truth lost in those days would apply to truth the Lord is restoring today.

Is there anything of greater value than the life, suffering, death and resurrection of Jesus? The reply of every born again Christian would be that *nothing* is of greater worth. This is certainly true from a human perspective, considering our great need as sinners to satisfy the righteous judgments of a Holy God. However, from God's perspective it is *not* the correct answer. The value to Him in what He purposed to accomplish was based on knowing, from the very beginning, the terrible price He would pay to achieve it. To Him, the value was greater than the cost! The glory of His future tabernacle among and in men; the city of God; the place of His eternal rest constitute this value. Therefore, the purpose of God should be the primary motivation and goal of *all* ministry in the church. How well she is equipped for service in the days ahead and for her final destiny of reigning with Christ is the issue in church restoration. For this reason, an outline is presented of the scope of ministry that is required to equip saints for their place and work of service in the body of Christ during the crucible of testing that completes this age.

CHAPTER 1

WHERE ARE WE TODAY?

But you, brethern, are not in darkness, that the day should overtake you like a thief. (I Thess. 5:4)

Let us rejoice and be glad and give the glory to Him, for the marriage of the Lamb has come and His bride HAS MADE HERSELF READY. (Rev. 19:7)

Repent therefore and return, that your sins may be wiped away, in order that times of refreshing may come from the presence of the Lord; and that He may send Jesus, the Christ appointed for you, WHOM HEAVEN MUST RECEIVE UNTIL THE PERIOD OF RESTORATION of all things about which God spoke by the mouth of His holy prophets from ancient time. (Acts 3:19-21)

A great many Christians are looking for the Lord to return at any moment. It is correct to have such expectancy. However, if we recognize that He is coming for a glorious, overcoming church, for a spotless bride then our hearts need to be adjusted to see that a crucible of purification is needed to restore and prepare the church for that wonderful day.

FACING THE FUTURE

It is clear that one does not walk backward into the future. You would not know where you are going! Yet, without being aware of it, that is what many Christians are attempting to do.

When eyes are kept focused on what the Lord did in the past; when hearts are filled with memories and visions of yesterday; when minds are preoccupied with the orthodoxy of one's tradition, then there is great danger of being unaware of new revelations the Lord may be speaking to His people.

This is an issue that concerns our feet and our eyes. The *past* belongs to our *feet;* we are to walk in the light of *all* truth the Lord has given to us. However, the *future* relates to our *eyes.* We must keep them focused on Him and what He is *speaking today* concerning the future. If we continue to gaze back into things of the past we will surely miss out in what is to take place. We can not back into the future; we must face it with our eyes on the Lord.

This leads us to a question that is frequently asked, "Where are we today according to the calendar of prophecy, and what is to take place next?" There are three distinct sets of observations one might use from scripture to answer this question.

First, we could consider all of Satan's activities in the world and compare them to what scripture has to say concerning evil in the last days. This could be considered as using a "calendar" concerning the adversary. Satan knows that his time is short and he is engaged in an all out effort to deceive and destroy every man, woman and child he can. Scripture warns of his tactics and schemes for these days. Thus, we need not be deceived by the false prophets and false Christs that will arise (i.e., New Age Movement, Unification Church, etc.), or be discouraged and pressed down in our spirits by increased lawlessness (i.e., crime, abortion, homosexuality, terrorism, etc.), or be led astray by new manifestations of deception from deceiving spirits (i.e., U.F.O.'s, astrology, witchcraft, E.S.P., etc.). Satan's strategy will eventually culminate in his incarnation in the man of sin. Those who favor this calendar spend much time trying to anticipate who this man will be, what nation he will come from and when he will appear.

Second, the regathering and restoration of Israel also represents a calendar that points to the soon return of the Messiah. It is significant that in 1988 Israel has been back in their land for one generation.

However, the most important calendar is to be found in the Lord's strategy to build and restore the church, preparing her for His return. We are to use *all* scriptures that apply to each of these three calendars; however, what the Lord is doing in and through the church must be given top priority as we move forward into the future.

To hear His voice amidst the rising noise and turmoil of voices from the world, to know what He is saying today to His people is more pertinent and profitable than using our best reasoning to interpret world events in the light of scripture. It is certain that the Lord's concern is not primarily on what Satan is doing, it is for His people! And that is where our attention should be focused as well.

A good example of failing to apply this priority, while placing too great an emphasis on Israel, is the unhappy consequences of the many who believed a booklet, written by E.C. Whisenant, entitled, *88 Reasons Why The Rapture Will Be In 1988.*

Finally, in looking to the future I expect some places will experience the grace of God in divine visitation. When this occurs it will be clear that the blessed Holy

Spirit does not require any human help to do His work.

A tract record of the Welsh revival at the turn of this century gives the following evidence of the sovereignty of God: "Suddenly, like a tornado the Spirit of God swept over the land. Churches are filled; meetings ran day and night. Thousands were saved or recommitted to Christ. Prayer, testimony and singing would sweep over the congregations in torrents, but there was little or no preaching, no hymn books, no choirs, no organs, no collections and finally no advertising."

In the following pages, as various subjects are discussed it should never be forgotten that an equipped church is one praying for and expecting a spontaneous moving of the Holy Spirit. It is He alone who performs the work of God!

A TIME OF TRAVAIL

For the anxious longing of the creation waits eagerly for the revealing of the sons of God. For the creation was subjected to futility (i.e. emptiness, uselessness), not of it's own will, but because of Him who subjected it, in hope that the creation itself also will be set free from its slavery to corruption (i.e., decay, destruction) into the freedom of the glory of the children of God.

(Ro. 8:18-21)

Adam was made a perfect man to rule over a perfect creation, one that included all ecological life and all of the earth's resources. God placed Adam as lord over the earth.

When Adam sinned he relinquished lordship of the earth and became in his fallen state, a man of death. As such, he was out of place in the perfect creation. Very likely he could not sustain his life in creation as it existed then.

We don't know exactly how, but the Lord reached out and touched creation to make it compatible to Adam. He subjected it to futility. Creation did not wish this to happen but God acted in hope and expectation, that as man was eventually restored, so would creation also be restored. In the meantime, corruption would multiply through Satan's influence both in man and creation.

From that day until now there has been travail in believers and in creation for restoration. As this age nears its completion, both creation and the church are in travail waiting for one thing: the revealing or manifestation of God's sons coming into their place of authority in the earth.

God's plan is that since man was responsible for the fall, he must first be restored. After this takes place, being completed at the coming of the Lord, then creation would also be restored (Ro. 8:23).

Man's restoration will not occur in one or two super-spiritual individuals. It will be in the glorious church that the Lord is raising up; it will be His bride who is preparing herself for His return. For this reason, above all else, the hearts of believers should be centered on the Lord and His work of restoring the church.

RENEWAL AND RESTORATION

Church restoration, which began in the early sixteenth century with the teachings of Martin Luther and the Anabaptists, was a slow methodical phenomenon for approximately four hundred years. However, the Lord ushered in this century by restoring truth of "the baptism in the Holy Spirit," and because of His greater presence in the church, there has been an ever increasing acceleration of restored truth. The Lord is doing a *quick* work in righteousness as He prepares His body for the climactic events that will close this age.

The prophet Joel prophesied that a great outpouring of the early and latter rain of the Holy Spirit would restore the church to fruitful abundance in the end times. The Lord would make up for the years lost by what the swarming, creeping, stripping and gnawing locusts had destroyed in the church (Joel 2:23-27).

I believe that at no time has any individual Christian ever been denied the revelation and experience of a truth in scripture when they sought the Lord in faith with all their hearts. However, times of restoration to the church are in the heart of the Lord. For example, there have been individuals down through (apparently) every generation of the church who were baptized in the Spirit, but it wasn't until the beginning of this century that it was restored as truth to groups of believers in the body of Christ.

As a result of this particular restoration, the early part of this century was marked by more anointed ministries and restoration of the nine spiritual gifts.

The middle of the century saw the "Latter Rain" revival restore new dimensions of spiritual worship, and truth concerning the laying on of hands by a presbytery for prophetic confirmation of the calling and ministry gifts of individual believers. [3]

In the early 1960's, the charismatic renewal began spontaneously in which the Lord poured His Spirit out upon those who were receptive in many of the denominations that comprise Christendom. The results were mixed, from little response in some bodies, such as the Orthodox churches, to a remarkable acceptance by the Mennonite church. Most believers in these bodies sought for spiritual renewal of their particular denomination. In this way, many members entered into a richer and more fruitful walk with the Lord. It has also been the means of evangelizing those in these churches who were members in name only. This has been particularly true in the Roman Catholic church. However, renewal has been essentially confined to individual believers with little or no effect on the inflexible wineskins and authority structures of institutional churches.

During the charismatic renewal, various constraints to restoration of mainline churches became apparent in their traditions, doctrines and trans-local governments. Because of such things some men sought God for revelation on how to build strong, flexible wineskins that would contain and preserve the new wine being poured out. In response, the Lord began to raise up apostolic men with a burden and vision to follow the pattern of the New Testament church seen in scriptures and to build churches as local expressions of the body of Christ. The traditional clergy-laity distinction was replaced with an emphasis on the vital and unique place that *each* member is called to fill in the life functions of a local body.

The question arises, "how can valid apostolic and prophetic ministries help those bodies of believers who have hearts for the Lord's house and restoration of His church?" Unfortunately, many restoration movements have modeled their assemblies after churches of the second century more than after the churches built by Paul. To begin with, it is necessary to understand what took place, and what contributed to the initial decline of the first church. It is quite reasonable to expect that decline of the early church could mirror for us the restoration to come. That is, the "end of the beginning" (of the early church) would reflect "the beginning of the end" (for church restoration today). Let us see if this is so.

The following is a historical record of the first two

centuries of the early church as gleaned from the writings of a number of authors.

HISTORICAL RECORD OF THE FIRST CHURCH

1. A.D. 30-50. The church was birthed in Jerusalem on the day of Pentecost and grew very quickly in numbers. Peter, James and John stand out among the apostles. Peter's first epistle endorses plurality of elders (1 Pet. 5:1-3), Peter himself being one of the elders. A strong legalistic emphasis, seemingly encouraged by James, proved to be a hindrance to the church at Jerusalem.

John W. Kennedy in his book, *The Torch Of The Testimony* [4] writes as follows concerning the Jerusalem church, "Those in the church at Jerusalem found it much more difficult to disassociate themselves entirely from the tradition of Jewish ritualism, and this obsession with outward form ... was the beginning of the rot which was ultimately to corrupt the life of the church." (P 12)

2. A.D. 43-67. Paul was brought to Antioch by Barnabas, where they labored together and from where they were sent out to plant new churches. Kennedy makes the following comment on this period of time, "The focus of the Spirit's working was unquestionably shifting from Jerusalem to Antioch." (P 12)

The churches planted by Paul proved to be excellent local expressions of the body of Christ. His work and epistles contain the pattern for God's theocractic government of local assemblies.

The following are some of the characteristics of these churches that are evident from Paul's epistles:

- Ministry was spontaneous, prophetic and charismatic.
- There was no clergy-laity distinction.

- Rather than organizational structure, local church emphasis was on family relationship and body life.
- There was no programmed meeting format; the Holy Spirit's control was sought.
- Men in leadership were primarily servants who ministered out of the grace and anointing resting upon them rather than from the authority of an office.
- Assemblies were autonomous, each one under the oversight of a collegial eldership who were responsible to shepherd and equip the saints.

3. The following are some documented references to this last item concerning local church government over approximately the first one hundred years.

- *The Didache* [5] (written by the first apostles.) This document, which was circulated among the early churches in the first century, made no distinction between elder, bishop or presbyter. (P 121)
- Dr. Bill Hamon in his book, *The Eternal Church* [6] states, "At the close of the apostolic age churches were independent of each other and shepherded by a group of co-pastors." (P 94)
- Kennedy makes the following comments on government of the early church: "The two Greek words translated as 'bishop' or 'overseer' *(Episkopos)* and 'elder' *(Presbuteros)* indicate the same office and are used interchangeably." (P 22) "The churches in early days were not linked by any type of federal organization although they were closely united by fellowship." (P 32)
- E. H. Broadbent in his book, *The Pilgrim Church* [7] states, "the word 'elders' is the same as 'presbyters', and the word 'overseers' is the same as 'bishops', and the passage (Acts 20:17-35) show that there were several such in one church." (P 8)

- Philip Schaff in his book, *History Of The Christian* Church [8] writes as follows, "the term 'presbyter' (or elder) and 'bishop' (or overseer, superintendent) denote in the New Testament *one* and the *same* office ... they appear always as a plurality or as a college in one and the same congregation ... the presbyters always formed a college or corporation presbytery ... they no doubt maintained a relation of fraternal equality." (PP 491-497)
- The writings of Clement of Rome [5] (A.D. 96) uses the words 'bishop' and 'elder' interchangeably. In his epistle to the Corinthians he writes, "Let us reverence our rulers; let us honor our elders", "submit yourselves unto the presbyters." (PP 1-41)
- The epistle of Polycarp [5] (A.D.110) to the Philippians lists essentially the same character requirements for the presbyters as do Paul's epistles. He opens this epistle by the words, "Polycarp and the presbyters that are with him". (PP 91-99)

4. In the days of Clement and Polycarp, there began to be references made of the presbyters as 'priests'. This became the first subtle step that eventually led to two classes of believers, clergy and laity. Polycarp and Clement recognized *only two* ministry groups in their churches, elders and deacons. By this time spiritual gifts had become less frequent in church meetings. The revelatory and charismatic emphasis was slowly being replaced by teaching and definition. It was a contemporary of Polycarp, Ignatius, Bishop of Antioch, who set the direction that would be embraced by churches in the second century. He amplified the distinction between clergy and laity. Each eldership had *one* member elevated as bishop to whom the other elders and church must submit. Thus, *three* leadership

roles began to replace elders and deacons of the early church.

Because of diminishing manifestations of spiritual gifts and ministries, especially apostles and prophets, control of church life passed more from the Holy Spirit to an office of leadership. The graces of servanthood and humility, which are essential in collegial elderships, became less important than a strong leader out of desire for more structure and a defined orthodoxy to defend against heresy.

The eventual consequence of the bishop's office is that it began to replace apostolic ministry of the first century in importance.

When bishops began to assume authority over neighboring assemblies of the region during the second and third centuries, another level of authority was put in place to represent these new assemblies to their bishop. This ministry office became known as "the pastor."

By now, elders were no longer the five ministries of Eph. 4:11, deacons were greatly restricted in their spiritual service, the body of Christ was divided into clergy and laity classes and assemblies were no longer autonomous.

5. The following are further references of the church during the second and third centuries.

- In his epistles, [5] Ignatius emphasizes the need for *one* strong elder to rule the presbytery and the church. He spoke of this as the office of the bishop or episcopate. He writes to the Ephesian church, "I have received your whole multitude in the person of Onesimus ... who is your bishop. Plainly, therefore, we ought to regard the bishop as the Lord Himself." To the church of Smyrna, Ignatius writes, "Let no man do aught of things pertaining to the church apart from the bishop ...

it is not lawful apart from the bishop either to baptize or hold a love-feast". (PP 63-68)

- Kennedy writes of the church in this period of time as follows, "From the point to which Luke conducts us in his history of ACTS until the latter part of the second century there is a conspicuous lack of historical information on the development of assemblies. When we emerge from this period of uncertainty, we find a church in many respects quite different from the churches of the New Testament. Wide and far-reaching changes have taken place, and there is an unmistakable move in the direction of the institutionalism of later years." (P 37) In this section of his book, Kennedy also makes an astute observation, one that every leader ought to take heed to: "whatever God establishes man ultimately wants to prune and shape to his own liking."
- L.P. Qualben, in his book *A History of The Christian Church* [9] writes, "during the second and third centuries important changes took place. Instead of government by a group of elders, local churches were headed by a single official for whom the name 'bishop' was exclusively reserved. The presence of the bishop was now essential to *every* valid act of the congregation. In fact, without a bishop there was no church". (P 96)
- Hamon writes, [6] "Gradually the jurisdiction of bishops came to include neighboring towns. Bishop Calixtus was the first bishop to base his claim on the scripture Mt. 16:18. Tertullian called Calixtus an usurper for speaking as if he were 'bishop of bishops.' " (P 94)

5. The following five men were the most prominent church leaders bridging between the second century

and close of the Ante-Nicene era (A.D. 175-325): Irenaeus; Clement of Alexandria; Tertullian; Origen and Cyprian. During this period, rule by a monarchial bishop was fully established. Thus, hierarchical government in the church became engrained in Christendom where for the most part it remains until today despite much progress in restoration. Later when the bishop of Rome came to have preeminence over the other bishops he was termed "the first among equals."

One of the most widely accepted authorities on the history of the church is the famous theologian and scholar J.B. Lightfoot. His essay entitled, THE CHRISTIAN MINISTRY [13], written in 1868 contains an excellent exposition on the evolution of the original two ministries (elders and deacons) of the early church into the three ministries (bishop, elders and deacons) of the second and third centuries.

Certainly, the difference between Pauline churches and the church two hundred years later is most clearly evident in the reduced role of the Holy Spirit. However, this could only have taken place because of increased control by those in leadership. For this reason, for complete restoration to take place, there must first arise a significant ministry of apostolic and prophetic men with hearts and vision like those of the first disciples.

They will be men who recognize that the Lord will return for a church wholly separated unto Him, one that He can present to Himself in "all her glory, having no spot or wrinkle or any such thing" (Eph. 5:26-27); a bride who has made herself ready! Therefore, they will be committed to all that pertains to her divine architecture and fullness.

Let us examine what scripture teaches concerning the qualities and functions of these two ministries.

CHAPTER 2

APOSTLES AND PROPHETS

And God has appointed in the church, first apostles, second prophets...

(1 Cor. 12:28)

There is a crucible related to leadership. It is the crucible of servanthood. Society frowns upon servants; everyone wants to be first, to be a leader! However, servanthood is the essential heart attitude for godly leadership. The heart of a bond-servant, not career training for professional ministry, is the Lord's qualification for leaders in His church. While true for leaders in general, this is particularly true for apostles and prophets who are jointly responsible for the foundation of local churches.

GIFTS OF THE LORD

And He gave SOME AS APOSTLES, AND SOME AS PROPHETS and some as evangelists and some as pastors and teachers, FOR THE EQUIPPING OF THE SAINTS FOR THE WORK OF SERVICE, TO THE BUILDING UP OF THE BODY OF CHRIST; UNTIL WE ALL ATTAIN TO THE

> *UNITY OF THE FAITH, and of the knowledge of the Son of God, TO A MATURE MAN, to the measure of the stature that belongs to the fulness of Christ.*
>
> (Eph. 4:11-13)

Commitment to God's purpose in our generation is a commitment to see the fullness of His power, character and glory displayed in the church. Such commitment must include a willingness on our part to embrace and walk in *all* the grace and truth Christ reveals to us for the building of His body. In particular, He has extended specific grace to five ministry gifts, whose joint purpose is to properly equip each saint for the work of service that God has called them to. Therefore, commitment to His purpose must include recognition of the need for each of these ministries. Unfortunately, two of them, apostles and prophets, whose service includes the laying of church foundations, have been neglected in much of Christendom.

Because these ministries are gifts from the Lord, it is vital that they represent Him faithfully in all that they do. If they believe they are more important than others, and dominate the flock they can do great harm. For this reason, the Lord deals with the hearts of His ministers on how they are to see themselves and how they are to represent, or present, themselves to others.

FIRST, SERVANTS

It is important how to present oneself when representing the Lord in ministry. How we appear in the eyes of our audience will condition their response to our message. A speaker with a proud, unbroken spirit will impart little life to others. However, even if one's heart is pure, it is possible to convey the appearance of pride by ministering out of the authority of a title or an office.

The Lord Jesus instructed His disciples on this issue as follows:

> *But do not be called Rabbi; for One is your Teacher, and you are all brothers. And do not call anyone on earth your father; for One is your Father, He who is in heaven. And do not be called leaders; for One is your Leader, that is, Christ. But the greatest among you shall be your servant.* (Mt. 23:8-11)

These verses focus on the human heart, and its potential to become tainted by pride. What a man builds by ministry he can destroy by his character; and more than anything else, pride will destroy the integrity of one's character. What we *are* in Christ, determines the quality of what we can *accomplish* for Him.

In institutions of the world, officials function out of the authority vested in their offices. As long as someone occupies an office, its function can be carried out. However, God does not operate in that manner; His disciples function out of the anointing He imparts to them. No anointing means no function! Leaders in the church are not primarily called to be decision makers; they are men who, because of the anointing and grace upon them, are able to hear from God and act accordingly.

The Greek word "EPISKOPE" in 1 Tim. 3:1, often translated as "office" means literally "an overseeing," and it implies one who is anointed by God for that function. In a secular application of the word, there are no offices in the church.

The first priority for one called to any of these five ministries is to develop the heart of a servant and to cultivate humility to grace his words. The importance of servanthood was a primary emphasis in the teaching (and example) of Jesus to His disciples:

> *You know that the rulers of the Gentiles lord it over them, and their great men exercise authority over them. It is not so among you, but whoever wishes to become great among you shall be your servant, and whoever wishes to be first among you shall be your slave; just as the Son of Man did not come to be served, but to serve, and to give His life a ransom for many.* (Mt. 20:25-28)

To some, such things as titles or offices may seem insignificant compared with other issues. They would say our only valid concern should be to preach the gospel by exercising all gifts and ministries of the Spirit. These believers seek one thing; to have the *acts* of God in their midst.

To others, such things are indispensable for an efficient running of church apparatus. They see the assembly functioning as a business organization, or a well oiled machine; it will only be efficient when properly controlled by capable men (or women) in offices with titles and resources to support their function. They primarily seek to define and control their work for God, whatever that may be.

Those who press on with the Lord in this time of renewing and restoring His church will discover that *everything* which does not conform to His character and word will be dealt with. They will see that titles and offices have no place in His house.

For example, the practice of prefacing a minister's name with the word "reverend" violates the Lord's commandment in Mt. 23:8-11. The word "reverend" comes from the Hebrew word YARE which literally means "awesome" or "awe-inspiring". Thus, it can *only* have reference to the Lord's name (Ps. 111:9). Imagine Paul signing his epistles as follows:

Respectfully yours,
The awesome (or right-awesome) apostle Paul.

Similarily, the title of senior pastor (or chief shepherd) is reserved only for the Lord Jesus. It is difficult to imagine any of the early disciples using such a title.

FUNCTION

The Lord's commandment to not use personal titles, such as teacher, father or leader, does not deny the validity of these functions. We are to father others in Christ, we are to teach them and, it given grace to do so, we are to lead them. However, our emphasis must be on the function given to us by the grace of God, not on a title.

How to do this becomes apparent when we discover how apostles of the early church identified their roles. For example, we find that Paul never referred to himself as, "the apostle Paul"; used in this manner, the word "apostle" would be a title. He always spoke of himself as "Paul, an apostle" which denoted his ministry function. In his epistles, Paul makes it abundantly clear that the authority and power of his apostleship came entirely from the grace of God; which of course is true for all ministry gifts.

Should God lift His grace and anointing from someone, the spiritual life in his ministry would instantly cease. However, if that person believed that his authority or right to minister came from his title, his office or the salary he earned from the church, he could go on ministering without God's anointing and not miss it. This would not only be harmful to the sheep, it would also dull his sense of accountability to the Lord. This is one reason why men in leadership must be free to speak to the presence or absence of grace in each another's lives.

When writing the epistles, five apostles in the New Testament identified their roles in the church through essentially four words. One word, bond-servant, defined their commitment to serve. The following three words expressed their ministry functions: apostle, master builder and elder. The following scriptures illustrate their use of these words:

1. Paul
   apostle: Rom. 1:1; 1 Cor. 1;1; 2 Cor. 1:1; Gal. 1:1; Eph. 1:1; Col. 1:1; 1 Thess. 2:6; 1 Tim. 1:1; 2 Tim. 1:1; Tit. 1:1.
   bond-servant: Rom. 1:1; Phil. 1:1; Tit. 1:1
   master builder: 1 Cor. 3:10
2. James
   bond-servant: Ja. 1:1
3. Peter
   elder: 1 Pet. 5:1
   bond-servant: 2 Pet. 1:1
   apostle: 2 Pet. 1:1
4. John
   elder: 2 Jn. 1:1; 3 Jn. 1:1
   bond-servant: Rev. 1:1
5. Jude
   bond-servant: Jude 1:1

The humility of these men of God is evident in that they saw themselves, first of all, as bond-servants of Christ. [10] They sought no self grandeur in titles or offices for they were following in the steps of their Lord.

Therefore, as valid apostles and prophets are raised up we can expect them to be men who see and present themselves as these five men of the early church did.

IT IS A MATTER OF GRACE

Each ministry gift of the Holy Spirit is uniquely a matter of God's grace. For example, no one can become a true pastor, evangelist, elder, deacon or exercise any spiritual gift apart from the grace of God. There is *no difference in greatness or importance* between giftings of the Spirit, there is only a difference in grace. This is dispensed as God sees fit, with each believer receiving a measure of grace for ministry.

> *And since we have gifts that differ according to the grace given to us, let each exercise them accordingly...* (Rom. 12:6)

> But to each one of us grace was given according to the measure of Christ's gift. (Eph. 4:7)

Paul was not intimidated or self-conscious when he identified his ministry by the word "apostle" because he knew it was *entirely* a matter of God's gift of grace to him.

> *But by the grace of God, I am what I am, and His grace toward me did not prove vain; but I labored even more than all of them, yet not I, but the grace of God with me.* (1 Cor. 15:10)

Grace establishes the sphere, or dimensions of one's ministry, as well as its specific character. This can be seen in Paul's apostolic ministry to the Gentiles.

> *If indeed you have heard of the STEWARDSHIP OF GOD'S GRACE WHICH WAS GIVEN TO ME FOR YOU: that by revelation there was made known to me the mystery ... that the Gentiles are fellow heirs and fellow members of the body, and fellow partakers of the promise in Christ ... I WAS MADE A MINISTER ACCORDING TO THE*

> *GIFT OF GRACE that was given to me according to the working of His power. TO ME ... THIS GRACE WAS GIVEN, TO PREACH TO THE GENTILES...* (Eph. 3:2-3, 6-8)

Whatever our allotment of spiritual resources, they are intended for the benefit of others. Therefore, we are *stewards* of God's grace according to the uniqueness of our gifting in Christ. This requires that each believer be responsible to recognize the nature and dimension of grace given to him or her.

> *As each one has received a special gift, employ it in SERVING one another, as good stewards of the manifold grace of God.* (1 Pet. 4:10)

It is important to note that grace does not promote or elevate the recipient; on the contrary, grace is given to those who recognize their personal inability and weakness. The Lord is glorified when His life flows out to others from vessels who are meek and lowly in heart. In fact grace is *never* given to the self-sufficient or proud in heart. Any lack of brokenness will limit the grace of God in a ministry.

> *For God is opposed to the proud, but gives grace to the humble.* (1 Pet. 5:5)

Only in the area of ministry is grace limited on an individual basis according to one's call in God (2 Tim. 1:9). Grace is extended *without measure to all believers* in the area of their character. There is sufficient grace extended for each convert to become like Jesus (John 1:16; Ro. 5:20; Eph. 1:4-8; 2:7-8). Whatever the level of sin or failure in a life or a church, there is *always* more grace available in Christ than there is sin!

Since grace is a sovereign dispensation by God, why are certain ministry gifts of the Spirit so often lacking in churches? One reason is that grace must be coupled with faith to bring forth the reality of a ministry. This is true both on an individual and assembly level. All of us are responsible to believe and obey what God reveals to us concerning our place and service in the body of Christ. If I am content with my own way and methods of service then I will not seek to know His call on my life. And if I do not seek Him I will receive no revelation. However, if I do seek the Lord, and He reveals His will and purpose for me, there must be active faith *on my part* in obedience for it to come to pass. Then, if members in the assembly receive my ministry, all is well. On the other hand, if there is unbelief present concerning the nature or content of my ministry there would be little or no benefit to others. Thus, faith at the *assembly level* is also necessary for the grace of any ministry to become a beneficial reality to that body; and this is particularly true for the ministries of apostles and prophets. Thus, the church needs to be instructed on how Christ manifests His life through such men, and how to recognize and receive their ministries.

In summary, ministry originates in and flows from the grace of God by faith; ministry is qualified (or disqualified) by the character of the minister. It can also be hindered by unbelief in those being ministered to.

THE STANDARD

Many today in society do not want standards of righteousness imposed upon them; their cry is, "if it feels good, do it." However, God has established standards, not only for moral conduct but for ministry as well.

Too often we look back to prophets of the Old Testament as a means of defining the role and requirements of prophets in the church today. Similarly, we attempt to characterize what a New Testament apostle should be and do by Paul's ministry. There are valid lessons to be learned from these examples, especially from Paul; however, they are *not* the standard by which we are to measure. The Lord Jesus is the *one* and *only* standard for prophets, apostles and *all* other ministries.

The five-fold (or ascension gift) ministries listed in Eph. 4:11 are Christ's gift *of Himself* through men to the church. The diverse anointings upon these ministries are given to unveil the fullness of Christ to His people and to equip *each* member for service in order to bring the church to maturity. Every man called into one of these ministries must look to Jesus for *all* calibrations of his life and ministry. If we look at some successful man of God and try to emulate him, we will certainly come short in what Christ has called us to be and do. We might appear successful in the eyes of men but not in the eyes of God. Since the Lord Jesus has given these five ministry gifts to benefit *all* of His people, they belong to the whole church and never only to some group or denomination. Each of His ministers, especially apostles and prophets, need to possess a vision of the "one body in Christ" in order to avoid such things as sectarianism that divides believers into factions.

Let us consider how Jesus is the standard for prophets and apostles.

Moses prophesied that when the Christ would come, He would be a prophet to Israel having a significance to the nation like he himself had, in that the people must believe His words (Deut. 18:15; Acts 7:37). Peter identified Jesus to be this prophet by referring to the words of Moses.

Moses said, "The Lord God shall raise up for you a prophet like me from your brethren; to Him you

> *shall give heed in everything He says. And it shall be that every soul that does not heed that prophet shall be utterly destroyed from among the people."* (Acts 3:22-23)

Jesus Himself confirmed that He was a prophet.

> *Jesus said to them, "a prophet is not without honor except in his home town, and in his own household." And He did not do many miracles there because of their unbelief.* (Mt. 13:57-58)

> *Nevertheless, I must journey on today and tomorrow and the next day, for it cannot be that a prophet should perish outside Jerusalem.* (Lk. 13:33)

The Greek word used for prophet in the New Testament is PROHETES, meaning "a forthteller of divine will." This word is composed of two words, PRO meaning "before" and PHEMI meaning "saying" or "report."

The Hebrew word for prophet in the Old Testament is NABI, which means "a spokesman." Thus, a prophet is, *first* of all, one who *speaks* for God. A Septuagint word ROEH is translated in the Old Testament as "seer" in place of prophet. The use of this word did not imply insight, but rather hearing from God through visions. In essence then, a prophet is one who is anointed to receive, (perhaps by vision), and to speak forth the divine will of God.

The quality, or degree of excellence, in a prophet's ministry can be measured by three things:

1. the accuracy of what he says.
2. the content and timeliness of his messages.
3. how well his person endorses the truth of what he says; i.e., that his life and conduct does not discredit what he speaks for God.

On this basis, Jesus is the *one* true standard for a prophet's ministry. He spoke only *what* His Father gave Him to speak, and only *when* and *to whom* the words were intended; and the *manner* in which He spoke expressed His Father's heart. His total person and life were so much a part of what He proclaimed, that He was called "The Word of God." There was literally nothing that Jesus did or said that was without significance to the purpose of God.

When we examine the word "apostle" we discover that it means "one sent on a mission." Thus, if I send a child to deliver a message to my neighbor, his task could be termed apostolic. It is apparent that one's apostolicity in the Lord's work is a measure of two things:

1. who does the sending.
2. what is the mission.

Jesus did not come to earth on His own initiative, but was sent by His Father (Jn. 5:36-38; 6:29,38,44,57). His apostolic mission, insofar as the church is concerned, is expressed in the following verse:

> *...upon this rock I WILL BUILD My church...* (Mt. 16:18)

Through the Holy Spirit, men may be fellow-workers with Him in the building process, but Jesus is the One who really builds the church. First of all, He became the corner (or foundation) stone through His death on the cross; and second, He is the architect and builder of *all* that is placed on that stone. For this reason, He is *The Apostle* of His Father's House.

> *Therefore, holy brethren, partakers of a heavenly calling, consider Jesus, the APOSTLE and high priest of our confession. He was faithful to Him who appointed Him, as Moses was also in His house. For He has been counted worthy of more*

glory than Moses, by just so much as the BUILDER OF THE HOUSE has more glory than the house. (Heb. 3:1-3)

It was this vision of the future house (or city) of God that the Holy Spirit built into the heart of Abraham over the years of his relationship with the Lord.

For he (Abraham) was looking for the city which has foundations, whose ARCHITECT and BUILDER is God. (Heb. 11:10)

There are more references in scripture to the Lord's house than there are to Him as a shepherd. The Lord is *first of all* apostolic in His ministry. He is a builder!

The words, "building up" and "edification," in the New Testament are made up of constructs from two Greek words "DEMO": to build, and "OIKOS": a house, i.e., 1 Thess. 5:11; Eph. 4:12,16. Thus, the ministry of anyone sent by the Holy Spirit to strengthen and edify an assembly could be termed apostolic. Clearly, such a ministry might by teaching or evangelistic in orientation even though building is implicit in the ministry process.

However, Paul describes an apostle's ministry by the word "master builder" (1 Cor. 3:10). This is translated from the Greek word ARCHITEKTON from which we obtain our English word "architect." One would not start to build a house without first having a set of approved detailed drawings. Thus, the architect's function must precede that of the building contractor. ARCHITEKTON is composed of two root words in Greek, one meaning "to begin," and the other meaning "craftsman." This is precisely what an apostle's ministry is in the church. He is one sent by the Lord *to begin* building a local expression of the body of Christ. The grace of God resting upon him is in his anointing to know what must be laid foundationally upon the cornerstone in order for the Lord to build in the Spirit that which He purposes to do. After the foundation is laid, each man must then be careful how he builds upon it (1 Cor. 3:10). The subsequent building process could continue even until the Lord returns. It is important, therefore, that the foundation laid be accurate and complete in anticipation of all that lies in the future.

The Greek word in Heb. 11:10 which describes Jesus as the *architect* of God's house is TECHNITES, another word meaning "craftsman." This word, in turn, comes from a primitive root word meaning "to beget." Thus, Jesus as the Apostle of the church both *gave birth to it* (i.e., begat it) and is the One who is *building it.* The self-sacrifice, perfection and faithfulness in how He has given Himself to do this is the standard of *all* apostolic ministry in the church.

THE FOUNDATION OF APOSTLES AND PROPHETS

When one lays a foundation and constructs a building upon it, the resulting structure will be determined by the intended purpose of the building. For example, a tool shed will not be like a penthouse, neither will a child's tree house be like a garage, or a barn like a chicken-house. The purpose defines the structure, which in turn dictates the foundation. Thus, the proper foundation for a house will depend on its purpose.

There are numerous groups of believers who have affiliated as legal churches around some Christian endeavor related to the gospel. The question is, what foundation are they built upon? If they are true believers then, as such, they have built their individual lives upon the Lord Jesus Christ. They belong to Him, and He is a sure foundation for their faith. However, this personal relationship alone is *not* a sufficient foundation for their collective relationship as a church. The foundation of their church body is a matter of the committed purpose around which they have come together. For example, when it is based on meeting some specific need rather than the whole purpose of God the foundation will be lacking.

The Lord has *one* central purpose for His house; it is to be the place of His presence. *[11] It is to become His dwelling place where He can express the fullness of His glory to all creation. Other goals are secondary and must flow out of this purpose. When a foundation is laid for a local church, and is truly based on His purpose, it will be what scripture terms, "a foundation of apostles and prophets." Implicit in this foundation will be *all* the fundamentals of salvation such as grace, faith, repentance, water baptism, spiritual gifts and ministries, prayer, worship, family order, fellowship, etc. However, in the end, the importance of these truths is not simply in the amount of knowledge they represent, but how well they serve to build together the saints into a suitable dwelling place of God through the Spirit.

Apostles and prophets are *not* themselves the foundation of a church; rather the foundation is what they establish through their ministries in building the saints together as a functioning local expression of the body of Christ.

> *For through Him we both (Jew and Gentile) have our access in one Spirit to the Father. So then you are no longer strangers and aliens, but you are fellow citizens with the saints, and you are of God's household, HAVING BEEN BUILT*

* *11: pp 57-75*

UPON THE FOUNDATION OF THE APOSTLES AND PROPHETS, Christ Jesus Himself being the cornerstone, in whom the whole building, being fitted together is growing into a holy temple in the Lord; in whom you also are being built together into a dwelling of God in the Spirit. (Eph. 2:19-22)

The above verses are an excellent encapsulation of the essence of salvation. Some may argue that these verses will only be fulfilled by the universal body of Christ in the future and they abdicate any responsibility for them today. However, the city that the Lord will dwell in one day on earth is *being built* today from living stones in local assemblies; *it is important how* we build today if we are committed to the purpose of God. There are four pillars of truth expressed in these verses that establish His purpose:

1. Those who have been redeemed through the blood of Christ have access in one Spirit to the Father (i.e., there is *only one way* and *one access* to God).
2. This one access brings believers into a family relationship with *all* other believers (i.e., there is *only one family or one body* of believers, and *one covenant* uniting them).
3. The house of God is built upon a foundation laid by apostles and prophets, which rests upon Christ Jesus as the cornerstone (i.e., there is only *one foundation* for the house of God).
4. The Holy Spirit is working in assemblies all over the earth, fitting members together as living stones to build local expressions of His house. Out of what has been built through the Spirit, God purposes to bring together in the future His dwelling place among men, the place of His rest from which His government will go forth over the earth, and from which the fullness of His glory will be displayed forever

(i.e., this is the *one purpose* of God that undergirds all ministry). Our inheritance in His glory is where our heart should be centered (2 Thess. 2:13-14; Eph. 1:11; Ro. 8:28-30).

Practical implications of the above truthes are worked out in the "nitty-gritty" aspects of life and fellowship of local churches. We are saved through an individual decision and commitment, however, we will only fully come into our inheritance in Christ by being built together in local expressions of His body. When we learn to love one another, when we develop patience, long suffering, gentleness, compassion, forgiveness and learn to serve others, we provide the spiritual material out of which our dwelling place in the house of God is built. What we build today, we will live with for all eternity! It is one thing to be saved; it is another to have a place of glory in His house. Our abode in God's house will be built of the spiritual materials we send up today!

Each of us has been created with deficiencies that only God can satisfy. What we need may come to us by a sovereign impartation from the Lord, or He may minister to us through brothers and sisters with whom we have been relationally built. It is the issue of life. Structure, and thus the foundation, must be such that there is no hindrance to the flow of life from the Lord to members or between members in their relationship and ministry to each other. What emerges spiritually as structure in an organizational or governmental sense will be the result of this life flow. If structure hinders this flow, then the structure is wrong! And if the structure is wrong, the first place to look for faults is the foundation. A common mistake in this area is to organize believers around hierarchical levels of authority modeled after command structures of the military or secular business world. Man can optimize *his control* by imposing levels of authority, but *only* at the cost of disrupting the horizontal bonds of life built by the Spirit between members. This we *must not do!*

There is no one in the body of Christ without value in God's eyes. By the power of the Holy Spirit, and faith in the word of God, even the least promising individual can be saved from sin, be healed in their emotions from the consequences of sin to become a unique expression of God's love and life. It is by the integrated total from each individual contributing member that the Lord's life is fully expressed in an assembly. The body of Christ, as well as God's creation of flowers, birds, animals, planets, gems, etc. all point to great diversity. *Diversity* expresses the heart of God, and particularly so in the church! Only through the multiple diverse anointings of the five-fold equipping ministries can each member in a local church be taught, shepherded, built up in the faith, brought into relationship and established in righteousness, so that they attain to the place of service they have been called to in Christ. A correct foundation is one that anticipates and promotes this diversity; a human foundation leads to religious conformity and man's control.

God's divine architecture for a local church is revealed in the pattern He gave Moses for building the Old Testament tabernacle. **10* For example, qualities of the Spirit that bond believers together in an assembly are foreshadowed in the material and construction of the tabernacle walls (Ex. 26:15-30).

Wood is a type of human nature, just as gold speaks of God's nature. The boards used to build the walls were approximately twenty-seven inches wide and fifteen feet high. They were cut from the Acacia tree, whose wood was very hard and gnarled. Great skill

*10: pp 123-148

and resource were required to trim and plane these boards so that they were perfectly straight with smooth surfaces. This attention to detail was necessary so that straight uniform walls would be constructed. When a board was completed it was covered with a thin layer of gold. The amount of work required to finish each board points to the great task of the Holy Spirit in transforming our natures, twisted and gnarled from the consequences of sin and going our own way, into righteous natures that reflect the indwelling of Christ (i.e., the covering of gold). Each board was finished so that it could be mounted in a tightly coupled fashion to the two boards adjacent to it. This union points to the truth that we are members of one another and that God seeks to build us together through a fellowship of life in the Holy Spirit. We are *not* independent of one another. Each one of us has been fashioned to fit a special place in the body that has been prepared just for us.

However, more than the vertical boards is required to make an assembly strong enough in the Spirit to withstand the destructive pressures of outside forces that come against it. Five wooden bars, which were also finished smooth and covered with gold, were mounted in a parallel, horizontal fashion along the outside surface of the wall. These bars gave to the wall the supporting strength and stability necessary to stand firm. The bars speak of the five-fold ministries of Eph. 4:11 and their importance to the spiritual strength and unity of a church. Their horizontal position points to the fact that they are servants; they are mounted so as to serve the other boards. One of the bars ran the entire length of the wall, being in contact with each board. This speaks of the foundational ministry of an apostle. Whoever is called "to be one of the these five bars" must be prepared to have the Lord trim, smooth and sandpaper him in order to fit him into the place He has been called to serve. However, he has not fully arrived in his ministry if he is not yet *"covered with gold."* It is one thing to be called to a ministry; it is another thing for every one in the church to recognize the grace of the Lord Jesus resting upon him. The gold of God's character must be seen!

When we examine the record of how the apostle Paul laid foundations of churches, we find that his final step in completing a foundation was the appointment of elders to oversee and shepherd the assembly (Acts 14:23; Tit. 1:5). This plural company of men, along with traveling ministries, become the source of the five bars for that particular wall (or church). The gold covering of the bars foreshadows character qualifications for elders (Acts 20:17, 28-35; 1 Tim. 3:1-7, Tit. 1:5-9).

God's government is an integral part of the foundation. The most important element is the lordship of Christ in individual lives. Church government must *never* usurp this aspect of a Shepherd-sheep relationship. However, the Lord's government of His people in a *collective* sense lies with those overseeing the church. The answer to the following two-part question will help distinguish between what scripture teaches, and what is generally practiced in traditional churches concerning church government:

1. Why does the Lord assign responsibility for all oversight and shepherding of a church to elders, but places responsibility to equip the saints upon the five ministries listed in Eph. 4:11?
2. Why are detailed character qualifications given for elders, and yet not for these five ministries?

The only rational answer to this question is that elders in the Bible were chosen from men with these ministry gift callings. *10 What is often seen as elders in traditional churches today should not be confused with New Testament elders.

The significance of five bars reveal that more than the ministry of one man is required to oversee an assembly and equip the saints. The diversity of a five-fold ministry is required. Thus, the elders should not be clones, but be unique from one another in the grace and anointing of their ministries. Each must recognize the different grace resting upon his peers. They are to stand as *one man* in the responsibility of oversight, but they *will differ* in the grace and authority of their ministries. It will generally be sometime after the first elders are set in place over a new church before all of the fivefold ministries emerge in an eldership. This is one reason for the need of traveling ministries to help equip the saints.

THE CHURCH: A PROPHETIC PEOPLE

When the Lord communicates with man, the language of the Holy Spirit is revelation. In our humanity there is no way we could have articulate communication with God anymore than one of our household pets could speak with us. For this reason, God "translates" by the Spirit of revelation when He speaks to us. Of course He has no problem understanding us regardless of language, for He not only recognizes our words, He also reads our hearts. Thus, nothing we say, or think of saying, escapes Him. We communicate with God in order to pray, worship and have fellowship; while He, in turn, reveals Himself and His ways to us that we might come into the fullness of our relationship as His sons. His person, His ways, and all that He has prepared for those who love Him, *cannot* be understood apart from revelation (1 Cor. 2:9-14).

* 10: pp 57-66

Revelation is *first* and foremost an unveiling of the glory and majesty of His Person; and it is from the true knowledge (EPIGNOSIS) of Him that *all* other revelation flows (Eph. 1:17-23). This begins with the LOGOS, or the revealed record of what God has declared to bee His will and purpose for men. Thus, revelation of Jesus begins by seeing Him *first* as the Word of God,, for everything came into being by the words of His mouth. He not only is the Word, but He is also the radiance of His Father's glory, the exact representation of His nature; He possesses *all* authority in heaven and on earth; He is before *all* things and by Him *all* things hold together; in Him *all* the fullness of diety dwells, and He is head over *all* things to the church. To the extent we know Him, we also will know the Father and realize what it means to be fellow heirs with Christ and to comprehend the hope of His calling and the riches of the glory of His inheritance.

Thus, the place to begin is by prayerful study and searching of His word which shall *never* pass away. It is the yardstick (or plumbline) by which every revelation is to be judged. In it are many magnificent promises which are intended, through faith on our part, to bring us into His likeness (2 Pet. 1:2-11).

Although it is true that scriptures are the word of God and are therefore alive, energetic and powerful, we must remember it takes the Spirit of God, Who breathed them into existence, to help us understand them. It is He who illuminates, enlightens, and gives divine insight and revelation to men concerning their content. And without His intervention and assistance man is left to his own natural reasoning and wisdom to understand a truly supernatural piece of literature ... the word of God. He alone causes the scriptures to convict, adjust, inspire, and energize a believer's life so as to change him forever.

As Christians begin to live and walk in truth, they become a prophetic people to the world. The Lord's purpose is that they become a people living in the darkness of the world in such a way that their words, their lives, their relationships and ministries are a prophetic light to men and nations. God seeks to make His word flesh in His people, so that in them, the world can understand the nature, works and purpose of God. Through them the word of the Lord will expose lies coming from the confusing Babylon of voices of false teachers, spirits of deception, human ideologies, etc.

The unfolding plan of the Lord for His church can only be attained if *every* member is equipped for the specific place of service and calling that the Lord has ordained for them. Each of us has inherent deficiencies in spiritual abilities and understanding that makes us dependent on what our brothers and sisters have been given in the Spirit. Implicit in such supply is the Spirit of revelation, which is manifested through a variety of gifts and ministries. It is through this manifold diversity of prophetic manifestations that the Lord reveals Himself and His way through His many membered body. Some specific revelatory ministries are the following: the word of knowledge, the word of wisdom, the discerning of spirits, ministries of the word, spiritual songs, dreams, visions, the gift of tongues, the gift of interpretation of tongues, and finally prophetic utterances. Although all are necessary, and none are to be considered unimportant, yet preaching and prophecy occupy unique places of importance in bringing revelation to the church, and through her to the world.

There is always a time factor in the realm of prophecy. The church today is not where she was in the last generation. She is in transition! Since the late 1940's, God has been speaking much concerning restoration of apostolic and prophetic ministries. We are nearing the time when all will have been restored, and the Lord will come for His church. In prophecy, God speaks to us on the basis of *where* we are in time, and in the context of *what* He is doing *in our day.* For this reason, as a prophetic people, our lives and ministries should clearly point to the significance of the days in which we are living.

THE MINISTRY OF A PROPHET

There are three levels (or dimensions) of prophetic utterances in the church. First, every Spirit filled believer can manifest the *spirit of prophecy* (1 Cor. 14:31; Rev. 19:10). This aspect of prophecy essentially exalts the Lord Jesus, revealing His heart to the people and exhorting them to respond to Him and to one another.

> *For you can ALL prophesy one by one so that all may learn and all may be exhorted.* (1 Cor. 14:31)

Secondly, there is the *gift of prophecy* which is only given to some believers. This gift would generally have a more extensive message content, one that is intended to edify, exhort and comfort (1 Cor. 14:3).

Thirdly, there is the ministry of a prophet. [12] This ministry will occur less frequently than the gift of prophecy. The prophetic content of messages will be more substantial, and can include directive or confirmatory words related to the lives, ministries and decisions of others, as well as events or circumstances that concern the church. Three examples of a New Testament prophet's ministry are found in the following scriptures: Acts 11:27-28; 13:1-4; 21:10-11.

When I speak of a prophet, I am *not* referring simply to one who has this particular call on his life, but of one who fulfills the requirements of an elder, and who ministers out of relationship with, and accountability to, other elders in a local presbytery. Their ministry will endorse the following guideline and constraint:

> *And let two or three prophets speak, and let the others pass judgement.* (1 Cor. 14:29)

The fact that a man prophesies often in church does not make him a prophet. It is important not to publicly set in place an emerging ministry prematurely, not only for his sake, but also for the sake of the church.

When prophets are resident in a local church they are part of the eldership. When they travel translocally they are to be seen and received in the light of their particular ministry gift. In both cases, they prophesy out of the burden of the Lord. This does not mean that an elder who prophesies is necessarily a prophet; or that one called to be a prophet is yet an elder.

> *He who receives a prophet IN THE NAME OF A PROPHET shall receive a prophet's reward...* (Mt. 10:41)

An example of such dual identity is found in the church at Jerusalem. Acts 15:22 identify Judas and Silas as elders in the local church; verse 32 shows that they were prophets in their traveling ministries. Similarily, Peter was an elder and an apostle (1 Pet. 5:1).

When a prophet, or any other minister, is released to travel from an assembly, it means that he has been *sent* by the Lord and *released* by the church. In general, he will not travel alone, but in a team which in time will return and be accountable to the church and elders who released them for their mission (Acts 14:26-27).

It is in this context of translocal ministry that the prophets work jointly with apostles to lay foundations for new churches. The significance of their ministry is such endeavors can be summarized as follows:

1. Because of specific revelation(s) a prophet is able to *clearly express* God's heart on issues that are pertinent to the embryo church. Some possible examples could be: identifying a "strong man" that Satan may have placed over the area; corrective prophecies concerning hindrances in the life of one who the Lord is calling into His service; identifying or confirming the gifts and callings of certain believers; hidden sin; unknown circumstances that could cripple the work of God if not recognized; ungodly relationships that must be broken, etc.
2. He will bring a sharp clarity and emphasis to the word of God taught by apostolic and other ministries. Because of this aspect of his ministry, he is able to inspire believers to commit themselves to the purpose of God. His ministry will usually direct a pointed focus on important details and priorities.
3. He will impart to the people clear understanding of the time they are living in with respect to what God is speaking and doing in the church overall, and in particular, to what He is doing among them. In directive and predictive words, he will *not* point the people back to traditional roots, but he will point them to the present and future (Is. 42:9; 43:18-19).
4. He will minister as a bond-servant; one who is willing to lay down his rights and privileges for the sake of the gospel. He will *not* be known as one who *dominates,* but as one who *serves.*
5. The integrity of his character will be an example of the life and righteousness he is seeking to bring the people into. He will emphasize the relevance of character to ministry in the lives of the saints. A mature prophet will be able to point to difficulties, problems, circumstances, persecutions, afflictions, and misunderstandings that he has been brought through by the Lord in order to prepare him for his ministry.

6. When a prophet speaks for God, his words carry two things: the *thoughts* and the *heart attitude* of the Lord. Speaking correct words with a wrong spirit can devastate the hearers. A harsh, demanding, condemning voice instead of a gentle pleading would totally misrepresent the Lord. Therefore, if he is to minister grace, a prophet *must* be one who rules his spirit well (Pr. 16:2,23,24,32).
7. A prophet's ministry can be directive, not only for individuals, but also for assemblies; furthermore, some prophets will have directive words for national leaders and even for nations.

Surely the Lord God does nothing unless He reveals His secret counsel to His servants the prophets. (Amos 3:7)

THE MINISTRY OF AN APOSTLE

An apostle is one chosen and sent by Christ, so that first of all, he is *an apostle of Christ* whom he represents. Thus, he is not the apostle for an organization. Secondly, he is one sent by the Lord as a fellow worker with Him, anointed as a master builder to lay foundations for new churches (Gal. 1:1; 1 Cor. 3:9-10). Therefore, he is sent *to the whole body of Christ* and not only to some group or denomination. The two factors, "who sends him" and "what is his mission" determine and qualify his apostolicity.

The following items are the major spiritual parameters and functions of an apostle's ministry:

1. He is the "beginning craftsman," or architect, in the building process of a new church, and the authority of his ministry lies in his anointing. He is *not* more important than other ministries, he is simply *first in a time sense* for ministry in the building phase of a new church. He will recognize the strategy of the Spirit for the church in that area.

2. Until elders are designated, he possesses the responsibility and authority for what is being built, including the initial appointment of the elders. Such apostolic ministry may not be one person but several. For example, Paul and Barnabas were apostles who traveled as a team, as were Paul, Timothy and Sylvanus (1 Thess. 1:1,6).
3. Apostles are raised up within the eldership of local churches from which, in time, they will be released to travel and to whom they will be accountable.
4. An apostle is to recognize the sphere of his ministry and not go beyond it (2 Cor. 10:13-16). Such spheres may vary widely and change over time. For example, one could be sent to a foreign land with different culture and language. Here he would be responsible to raise up and train apostolic men within that culture to build the house of the Lord. Another man may be sent only to a small nearby region, a sphere that could expand as a result of his faithfulness and because of fruit in what is built. In all cases, an apostle should recognize the limitations of where he is sent, and *let the Lord expand it in His time.* A carnal desire for size, numbers and recognition can become a great stumbling block to men of God.
5. Apostles and prophets have grace for insight by revelation into the mystery of Christ (Eph. 3:4-5). This insight is manifest by the prophet in his anointing to sharply *declare the heart of God.* Prophets keep the saints from becoming "at ease" in Zion, and from getting stuck in the ruts of tradition. Such insight is revealed in an apostle's ministry by his ability in the Spirit to *communicate clearly the purpose of God* to the people by *written and spoken* words. His ministry of the word will be prophetic in content. He will bring an overall balance because he *sees the*

"whole picture" more clearly than do other ministries. Both ministries will know the priorities and emphasis of the Lord for the time and place where they live, and this will be reflected in their ministries. Above all else, they will exalt and reveal the Lordship of Christ.

6. Apostles (and prophets) will be men whose *authority is based on their character* and not on an office. It is not primarily a matter of how much authority one has, but rather, how well others recognize and submit to it. The Lord Jesus has all the authority of heaven and earth, yet He does not wield it as a big stick over our heads. Instead, He entreats us in love, out of all that He has done for us, to submit to Him. This is the pattern for exercising spiritual authority in the church. Love always calls for a response. This is how Paul's authority was established in his apostolic ministry, as is evident in his words to the churches he founded.

Nor did we seek glory from men, either from you or from others, EVEN THOUGH AS APOSTLES OF CHRIST WE MIGHT HAVE ASSERTED OUR AUTHORITY. BUT WE PROVED TO BE GENTLE AMONG YOU, AS A NURSING MOTHER tenderly cares for her own children—just as you know how we were EXHORTING and ENCOURAGING and IMPLORING each one off you AS A FATHER WOULD HIS OWN CHILDREN. (1 Thess. 2:6-11)

For you yourselves know how you ought to follow our example because we did not act in an undisciplined manner among you, nor did we eat any one's bread without paying for it, but with LABOR AND HARDSHIP WE KEPT WORKING NIGHT

> *AND DAY SO THAT WE MIGHT NOT BE A BURDEN TO ANY OF YOU.* (2 Thess. 3:7-8)
>
> *Here for the third time I am ready to come to you, and I will not be a burden for you; for I do not seek what is yours but you; for children are not responsible to save up for their parents, but parents for their children. And I WILL MOST GLADLY SPEND AND BE EXPENDED FOR YOUR SOULS...* (2 Cor. 12:14-15)
>
> You yourselves know that THESE HANDS MINISTERED TO MY OWN NEEDS AND TO THE MEN WHO WERE WITH ME. IN EVERYTHING I SHOWED YOU THAT BY WORKING HARD IN THIS MANNER YOU MUST HELP THE WEAK and remember the words of the Lord Jesus, that He himself said, "It is more blessed to give than to receive." (Acts 20:34-35)

The character of Paul, so evident in the theme of the above verses, was that of a bond-servant. Paul was as emphatic concerning his role as a bond-servant as he was about his ministry of an apostle. This bond-servant/apostle relationship is even more clearly seen in the earthly ministry of our Lord (Phil. 2:5-11). Therefore, apostles are to manifest godly character and righteousness before the people as a model for them to follow (1 Thess. 1:5-7; 2 Thess. 3:9; 1 Cor. 4:16). An apostle who would not be willing to support himself by secular work, if necessary, is a man who is not yet properly equipped for that ministry. The sure mark of a bond-servant's heart is that he seeks to serve rather than rule others. Such a man will not emphasize *his* ministry, but he will point to the grace off God. It can take years of the Lord's dealings to work the qualities of His heart into a man making him sufficient as a valid apostolic ministry. He will not be one who is highly acclaimed in the religious realm, for he will not fit into the mold of the status quo. Thus, the process of his training will involve misunderstandings and possible persecution. These, along with trials, tribulations, unpleasant circumstances, etc., will all be used by the Lord for good in building a stability and quality of character that qualifies his ministry.

7. There are four qualifications that mark an apostle; not simply one with this calling, but one whose ministry is evident through its fruit.
   - He will demonstrate the *grace* of God for such a ministry.
   - His integrity will be above reproach, and in particular, he will exhibit the *character qualities of a bond-servant.*
   - The *quality of what* the *Lord has built* through his ministry will prove him to be a master builder. He will be able to point to an assembly and say as Paul did:

     > *...For you are the seal of my apostleship in the Lord.* (1 Cor. 9:2)

     It is possible for a committed believer to lead people to the Lord, and in time to assemble a congregation under his oversight. Although he has fathered the work, this person is not necessarily an apostle. The quality of what has been built will reveal the grace of his ministry. Local churches are the interface of God's government to His people in a *collective* sense. What is built ought to have the structure God has ordained to facilitate His government. Therefore, it should not be an organizational hierarchy, but be patterned after the collegial eldership seen in the New Testament. The assembly should *not* be centered around the person or ministry of the founding apostle. Christ is to be central in the vision, ministry and government of the church. He should be free to act as Head over *all* things. When an apostle leaves a church he has founded and established, it should grow and prosper without him present.

- The fourth qualification is not unique to apostles, but should mark all who preach the gospel of the kingdom. There will be demonstrations of signs and wonders to prove that the gospel is true. Implicit in this will be a commitment to prayer and evangelism.

8. The manner by which apostles (and prophets) interface the churches they have founded will be *relational* and *not* governmental. This relationship would be much like a father relates to a son who had left home and his father's oversight to marry and raise his own family. The son is the one responsible for his family, but he could be greatly blessed by his father's input. When these ministries are invited to speak at other churches, they must come with hearts of *submission* to the existing leadership. Whether a pastor, senior pastor, or woman pastor is presiding; if God honors that leadership, they must also do so. apostles *do not* represent a level of authority over the local elders (or pastors in traditional churches). By demonstrating the grace and love of God through servants' hearts they should seek to establish organic bonds of trust and relationship with local leaders. In this way, the Lord Jesus builds His church on a regional basis.
9. Apostles (and prophets) will be men with hearts to train others in their ministry. A key strategy will be to take men in training with them on ministry trips for experience in real life situations and where trust and relationship can be built by their time together.

Finally, these two ministries must be prepared for the crucible of persecution, for they will *never* be popular with the world or inflexible religious establishments.

CONCLUSIONS

The following are four major conclusions:

1. Apostles and prophets are *essential* ministries for proper equipping of the saints, and for the building and maturity of the body of Christ. However, their service is *no more important* than the other ministries (1 Cor. 3:5-7).
2. The evidence of valid apostolic/prophetic ministries will be seen in the foundations laid for Biblical New Testament churches.
3. Apostles and prophets will be men who are qualified more by *character and commitment to Christ and His purpose,* than by supernatural acts of ministry.
4. The fourth is a personal conclusion. I believe the restoration of apostles and prophets will be a primary step from the many divisions and religious traditions of today to the united restored church that Jesus will come for. Although there are a growing number of prophets today there are few recognized apostles as yet.

It is easy to be caught up in a personal area of service for the Lord because of some need we see. However, it is *not* the needs of man, whether they are social, material or spiritual, but it is *the purpose of God* that is to direct us in ministry. There is a compelling demand today for men with compassion and mercy to minister to these needs, but they must be men with a foundational calling who have a vision of the purpose of God for these days. I believe the Lord is indeed raising up such men for all lands and areas of the world, including the nation of Israel; men who will bear the burden of the Lord for His church.

First the man, and then the message. Having considered these two foundational ministries, let us next examine the gospel they proclaim.

CHAPTER 3

THE GOSPEL OF THE KINGDOM

The Spirit of the Lord God is upon me, because the Lord has anointed me to bring good news to the afflicted, He has sent me to bind up the broken-hearted, to proclaim liberty to captives, and freedom to prisoners; to proclaim the favorable year of the Lord, and the day of vengeance of our God; to comfort all who mourn, to grant those who mourn in Zion, giving them a garland instead of ashes, the oil of gladness instead of mourning, the mantle of praise instead of a spirit of fainting. So they will be called oaks of righteousness, the planting of the Lord, that He may be glorified. (Is. 61:1-3)

The world today is being wooed by many competing voices expounding the merits of philosophies such as, secular humanism; mind altering drugs; Eastern Mysticism; E.S.P.; T.M; Unification theology; etc. Satan appears to be uniting these various deceptions under the umbrella of the New Age Movement. * The

* See Appendix, p 151

message that will defeat his strategy is the gospel of the kingdom.

Unfortunately, in many churches the gospel has drifted away from the whole purpose of God into various more limited emphases that focus on meeting specific needs. The fire of God's crucible is going to test and purify the gospel that is ministered in His house. There has been too much emphasis on who we are in Christ and not enough on who He is in us. In the gospel of the kingdom, His Lordship is far more important than the identity and function of those who make up His body.

THE LORD'S STRATEGY

The Lord's strategy for the last days is "a restored church with a restored gospel". A restored church without a gospel for the lost has no meaning. The Lord's purpose is centered in His bride but the burden of His heart is continually for the lost. If our vision and goal is to be the bride of Christ we must become a people who experience and share the burdens of His heart for evangelism.

One evidence that the church is not yet ready for her Lord's return is the many gospel emphases that are preached today. These include the social gospel, liberation theology, fundamentalism, the full gospel, faith and prosperity, reconstructionism, communalism, healing and deliverence, etc. Each of these are more oriented to man's needs than to the whole purpose of God.

The gospel is called "the gospel of the glory of Christ" (2 Cor. 4:3-4). It is when men lose sight of the supreme importance of the centrality of Jesus that they begin to focus more on gospels with other emphases.

THE ONLY GOSPEL

The gospel of the kingdom was the message Jesus

preached while upon the earth; it was the message He commissioned His disciples to minister to the house of Israel; it was the gospel ministered by the early church in the power of the Holy Spirit, and it is the message with which Jesus will consummate this period of the church age and bring about His return. He does not have one gospel for the unsaved, and another for the church; there is only one gospel. Therefore, it is vital the church understand that the gospel of the kingdom is her *one* and *only* commission.

Scripture is adamant that there is but one faith, just as there is only one body, one Spirit and one Lord (Eph. 4:4-6). Multiple and differing emphases of faith testify of multiple gospels; whereas one faith testifies of one gospel. There is only *one faith* because there is only *one gospel!*

The New Testament began with John the Baptist, who was sent to prepare the way of the Lord by calling the people to repentance and proclaiming that the time of the kingdom had come (Mt. 3:1-3,11).

The ministry of Jesus was wholly centered in the gospel of kingdom. This is particularly clear in the records of the synoptic gospels (i.e., Matthew, Mark and Luke). There were essentially three distinct components of truth in the gospel proclaimed by Jesus. These are the following:

1. He brought the good news of God's love and saving grace in the forgiveness of sins to the house of Israel. He called them to repentance, to believe in Him and follow Him.

> *... Jesus came into Galilee, preaching the gospel of God, and saying, "The time is fulfilled, and the kingdom of God is at hand; repent and believe in the gospel ... Follow me, and I will make you become fishers of men."* (Mk. 1:14-17)

2. He broke the power of Satan over the lives of those

who responded to Him (or desired to do so). In breaking demonic bondages He reclaimed many lives for God's kingdom who Satan had taken dominion over. His supernatural acts of healing and deliverence validated the truth of the gospel He preached (Is. 61:1; 1 John 3:8).

> *And Jesus was going about all the cities and villages, teaching in their synagogues, and proclaiming the gospel of the kingdom, and healing every kind of disease and every kind of sickness.* (Mt. 9:35)

> *And He went into their synagogues throughout all Galilee, preaching and casting out the demons.* (Mk. 1:39)

3. The kingdom of God is more than the forgiveness of sins and freedom from Satan's dominion; for those who embrace these first two steps it means to come under the Lordship of Christ and live victoriously above sin. It means to be relationally committed as a fellow citizen of God's household under the spiritual laws of His kingdom. Despite the absolute necessity and importance of the first two bodies of truth, the scripture record of this third component of the gospel of the kingdom is the largest of all three in our Lord's ministry. The context of His teaching is seen in the subject material of the beatitudes, the parables, the mysteries and the spiritual life principles of His kingdom. I suspect that these were a primary emphasis in what He taught His disciples concerning the kingdom during the forty days following His resurrection (Acts 1:3-6).

Some consider the gospels to be only "milk of the word" while the epistles are "meat of the word". This is not so, for the gospels are foundational for *all* that is contained in the epistles. Believers who are not established in the *simplicity* of the gospels will have *little depth* in the epistles, for both are the gospel of the kingdom.

All ministry of the Spirit is an expression of the kingdom of God. Whether one is anointed to lead a sinner to Christ, to counsel a believer, to teach children, to manage one's household, to exercise a spiritual gift, to preach, to shepherd, or to cast out demons, that individual is ministering the gospel of the kingdom. The gospel *always* serves to bring, or strengthen, the government of God in the lives of others.

Paul's ministry was the primary apostolic voice in building the early church, and his ministry was centered in the gospel of the kingdom (Acts 19:8; 20:25; 28:23,31).

The gospel is God speaking to mankind *in* His Son (Heb. 1:1-2). The gospel is not men speaking for God as prophets spoke in the Old Testament; the Son must be heard! To lay down our lives so that Jesus is seen and heard in our ministry, is to embrace the laws and principles that He spent so much time teaching His disciples about concerning the kingdom. Let us examine some of those life principles.

LIFE PRINCIPLES OF THE KINGDOM

Just as earthly kingdoms have laws to govern the conduct of their inhabitants, so these life principles are spiritual laws for the kingdom of God. Although there are many more, I have selected the following nine because of their importance to the success of evangelism and spiritual warfare.

1. The principle of *appropriation*.

   The "now word" God is speaking today everywhere, and especially in America, is "pray!" Persevering prayer is the strategy for appropriation; not prayer for general needs, but prayer that is forceful and demanding for doing spiritual warfare, and repentant and intercessory for needs of the church. Success in power evangelism, unity in the church, raising up apostolic and prophetic ministries, equipping believers for service, walking in victory under persecution, and becoming more like Jesus, *all* hang on this principle.

> *The law and the prophets were proclaimed until John; since then the gospel of the kingdom is preached, and everyone is FORCING his way into it.* (Lk. 16:16)

> *... ASK, and it shall be given you; SEEK and you shall find; KNOCK and it shall be opened to you.* (Lk. 11:9)

> *From the days of John the Baptist until now, the kingdom of heaven suffers violence, and violent men TAKE IT BY FORCE.* (Mt. 11:12)

The cost to bear burdens of prayer and appropriate victories in the kingdom is not small. It is pictured for us in the parable of a merchant who was seeking fine pearls; when he discovered one of very great value, he sold everything he owned in order to buy it (Mt. 13:44-45).

Appropriation can be based on corporate prayer when issues involve the church; or be a personal, or shared burden, for individual needs. In all cases, tears from broken hearts is a language that God understands. All worthwhile ministry begins with this principle. In particular, it is the foundation of evangelism.

2. The principle of *identification.*

   Each nation of the world possesses its own flag and official standard to establish the identity and citizenship of its inhabitants. Righteousness is the scepter (or flag) of the Lord's kingdom (Heb. 1:8).

> *A scepter of uprightness is the scepter of Thy kingdom* ... (Ps. 45:6)

Righteousness, and *only righteousness,* mark those who are children of the kingdom; ministry, doctrine, church membership or miracles do *not* prove one's citizenship in the kingdom of God. Jesus said His people are known by their fruit since a good tree cannot bring forth bad fruit, and a bad tree cannot bring forth good fruit (Mt. 7:16-24). The heart of God is to bring forth the fruit of His Spirit in each of His children, and to increase their fruitfulness through the often uncomfortable process of pruning (John 15; Gal. 5:22).

What a person builds in ministry, he can destroy by his character. Church history confirms this observation. Within the past century, there have been a number of men (and women) who were graced with extraordinary supernatural signs and miracles to accompany their preaching and evangelism. However, a relatively small percentage of them lived lives, that at times, were a reproach to the kingdom of God. Some of the flaws that became evident were: doctrinal error, divorce, drugs, drunkenness, exaggeration of results, exalted opinions of their ministry, luxurious living, and lack of financial accountability. Perhaps more than anything else, this record shows the error of individual ministries who function as "lone-rangers" with no accountability to others in the body of Christ. Such ministry is something less than the gospel of the kingdom.

In contrast, when the gospel is believed and embraced by a sinner it results in God's perfect righteousness being imputed to that person. As a new convert walks in the light of God's word, the righteousness of the Lord then becomes apparent in his life. He begins to show forth the glory of God. The greater the contrast with his old life; the more difficult the problems, circumstances or persecutions are in his new life, the more the glory of God will be seen in his witness. Too often we fail to recognize how God works in difficult circumstances to prepare us for a greater measure of glory. We fail to realize how our life adds to or takes away from the glory of God. The gospel we preach is greater than our words!

> *For whom He FOREKNEW, He also PREDESTINED to become conformed to the image of His Son, that He might be the firstborn among many brethren; and whom He predestined, these He also CALLED; and whom He called, these He also JUSTIFIED; and whom He justified, these He also GLORIFIED.* (Ro. 8:29-30)

The key verbs in the above verses are in the past tense; we *"have been"* glorified in Christ. Too often we become caught up with the importance of momentary issues and lose sight of the overall picture. Perhaps it is related to a trial we face, or we feel overwhelmed by an affliction or by the magnitude of some ordeal before us. God wants us to relate *everything* in our lives and ministries to His purpose, and rest in Him to bring His will to pass.
Whatever we encounter has been allowed into our lives to prepare us for His glory.

> *The Spirit Himself bears witness with our spirit that we are children of God, and if children, heirs also, heirs of God and fellow heirs with Christ, IF INDEED WE SUFFER WITH HIM IN ORDER THAT WE MAY ALSO BE GLORIFIED WITH HIM.* (Ro. 8:16-17)

> *For to you it has been granted for Christ's sake,*

> *not only to believe in Him, but also to suffer for His sake.* (Phil. 1:29).

Once we understand how we are being prepared for His glory we no longer need to be discouraged or surprised by tribulations and testings. They are our friends.

> *Beloved, do not be surprised at the fiery ordeal among you, which comes upon you FOR YOUR TESTING, as though some strange thing were happening to you.* (1 Pet. 4:12)

> *Therefore we do not lose heart, but though our outer man is decaying, yet our inner man is being renewed day by day. FOR MOMENTARY, LIGHT AFFLICTION IS PRODUCING FOR US AN ETERNAL WEIGHT OF GLORY far beyond all comparison.* (2 Cor. 4:17)

> *Because God has chosen you from the beginning for salvation through sanctification by the Spirit and faith in the truth. And it was for this He called you through our gospel, that you MIGHT GAIN THE GLORY of our Lord Jesus Christ.* (2 Thess. 2:13-14)

When the Bible speaks of God departing from a place, it is often expressed as, "the glory departing"; and His coming is often spoken of by phrases such as, "then the glory of God filled the place." When the Lord's kingdom comes in fullness the knowledge of the glory of God will cover the earth as the waters cover the sea. Thus righteousness and glory always mark the presence of Jesus whether in a place or a person. They are the *unique* qualities that identify those who make up His kingdom.

3. The principle of *judgement*.
This principle is closely related to the previous one.

Governments of the world judge the conduct of their citizens by how they obey the national statutes of laws. In the kingdom of God, saints are judged by the attitude and content of their hearts. For example, one may sin by committing a wrong deed, yet be judged lightly because his heart was good and he was ignorant of the situation. However, one who hates his brother is judged as a murderer, and one who lusts in his heart after a woman is judged as an adulterer in God's eyes.

> *But the things that proceed out of the mouth come from the heart, and those defile the man. For from the heart comes evil thoughts, murders, adulteries, fornications, thefts, false witness, slanders. These are the things that defile the man.* (Mt. 15:18-21)

As we are in our hearts at any moment, *is how God sees and judges us.*

> *As in water face reflects face, so the heart of man reflects man.* (Pr. 27:19)

Thus, to minister the gospel of the kingdom requires being diligent to guard and watch over one's heart, for the life of ministry issues forth from there (Pr. 4:23).

The word of God is described as a sharp sword of the Spirit (Eph. 6:17). However, it is not sharp simply because of accuracy and timeliness in what is spoken; it must also represent the Lord's heart attitude. If a word from the Lord is accurately given, but with a condemning spirit in the spokesman when the Lord intended soft gentleness to clothe his words, the result is not a sharp sword but a heavy, dull instrument that hurts and offends. The word of God in ministry must carry grace if it is to be redemptive.

Therefore, we have to minister the attitude of His heart as well as His words. It is a great help in this endeavor to have one's peers to evaluate our ministry; there can be valuable counsel in the wounds of a friend who might see something developing in our heart before we are aware of it.

4. The principles of *ministry*.

The previous three principles are key foundation stones that support spiritual ministry. There are three important characteristics of ministry. First, ministry is an impartation (or demonstration) of spiritual life; secondly, ministry to a member of the body of Christ is valued by the Lord as ministry to Himself (Mt. 25:34-40).

When a woman, who was ill with a hemorrhage, touched the Lord's garment in faith she was healed. Jesus immediately perceived that power had gone out of Him (Mk. 5:25-30). That was a ministry of healing, no different than if He had laid His hands upon her and prayed for healing. It is not the act itself, but what happens during the act, that constitutes ministry. For example, if a sick person goes to a practitioner of the occult for healing and is healed, that is *not* ministry; if an evil person, out of pity, gives a drink of water to another evil person who is thirsty, that is *not* ministry.

Ministry involves a flow of God's life in spiritual manifestations such as revelation, counsel, healing, teaching, spiritual gifts, confrontations and acts of love, etc. Such acts express the character and life of the Lord.

The third characteristic of ministry is that the unction and right to minister are resident in two keys of the kingdom (Mt. 16:19). These keys are *essential* to minister the gospel of the kingdom.

The first key is the *"power"* of God. This comes

from the presence of the Holy Spirit dwelling within our hearts (Acts 1:8). God's power is made perfect in our weaknesses (2 Cor. 12:9-10). If we are foolish enough to believe we can perform a ministry because of our ability, experience or knowledge, we will surely be disappointed. The Holy Spirit is our *only* source of power in the kingdom; furthermore, His capability to perform far exceeds our understanding (Eph. 3:20).

The second key is "the authority" of God. All authority in heaven and earth has been given to Christ (Mt. 28:18). Any authority one may have in the church has been delegated by Jesus from His authority. Those who submit to the will and authority of Christ will have grace to exercise authority in His name. However, it is not simply a matter of having authority, for it is only effective if others recognize and submit to it. The Lord's sheep do not submit readily to those who are dominating and authoritarian; they do respond to those who love and serve them (Ez. 34). Thus, a leader's authority is made perfect by his personal obedience and submission to Christ. This relationship of authority to character is evident in Paul's apostolic ministry (1 Thess. 2:1-2; 1 Cor. 9:11-27; Acts 20:17-20, 27-35). The authority of elders to oversee local churches is not given so that they can rule and dominate the lives of others; it is given to men, who because of their character, have the grace to feed, care for and serve the flock of God entrusted to them.

All believers because of their relationship to Christ, have authority to stand against Satan and his demons.

> *Submit therefore to God. Resist the devil and he will flee from you.* (Ja. 4:7)

Spiritual warfare has always been the normal environment for Christians, especially those who live godly in Christ Jesus. However, in the days ahead it will become more intense. The forces of darkness will become more pervasive and subtle through deceptive influence in the political and religious lives of men and nations. For example, I believe the New Age Movement will play a strategic role in Satan's attempt to deceive mankind. The kingdom of God cannot be built on earth without first tearing down Satan's kingdom. The Lord's church in an area can only be built from a place of authority in the heavens over that location. "Strong men" or princes of the enemy must be recognized and pulled down where ever the Lord's house is to be built.

For too long, most believers have been engaged in defensive tactics. Our major emphasis has been to do battle when we are attacked. We must make the transition to a strategy of attack! We have spent too much time in the barracks polishing our spiritual armor. Furthermore, we are to do battle knowing that the war has already been won, and that we are reclaiming for the kingdom that which has been wrongly usurped by Satan.

5. The principle of *mercy*.

Something besides words and great deeds is required to reveal the heart of God to mankind. Divine mercy expresses the magnificent dimensions of His love, supply and condescension to meet the needs of sinful men who are incapable of helping themselves. Mercy is a vital ingredient of the gospel of the kingdom, for without it the gospel would never be taken to places of great poverty, or persecution (e.g., Islamic nations), privation (e.g., prisons), ignorance, superstition and satanic oppression. Mercy is seen both in the message of the cross, and in those who lay down their lives to bring the message. One who weeps and travails for souls of the lost is one who has a heart of mercy. And this is indeed a generation to weep over when one considers the corruption and depravity in urban areas, and the lawlessness and rebellion against God that is pervasive everywhere. Nevertheless, the mercy of God is going to raise up many warriors for the kingdom from this generation of unsaved youth.

Practical implications of mercy are found in Luke's gospel (Lk. 6:27-36). Here we discover that those who minister the gospel are to extend mercy to their enemies, to those who hate them, who curse them, mistreat them, rob them and who then ask to borrow from them. To minister mercy is to express faith that God will redeem and change such individuals. Generally, one's first question is, "how can I become more merciful?" The *only* place to find mercy is at the throne of grace where it is dispensed (Heb. 4:16). It requires many trips and much time at the throne of His presence to become merciful. One thing that takes place here, is that we will develop a greater appreciation and understanding of the grace of God in our own lives. This helps us to be more merciful to others. Only in eternity will we really understand how great mercy was in the gospel that brought us into His kingdom.

Something that too often is neglected in Christian bodies is ministry to the poor. This becomes an important avenue for ministering the mercy of God. It is an *essential* component of the gospel of the kingdom. When John the Baptist sent word to Jesus asking Him if He were indeed the Messiah, the reply of Jesus revealed how His gospel of the kingdom validated His Messiahship.

> *The blind receive sight and the lame walk, the lepers are cleansed and the deaf hear, and the*

> *dead are raised up and the poor have the gospel preached to them.* (Mt. 11:5)

The Lord's emphasis on the poor is not simply that material needs are met, but in addition, because of their needs, the poor will more likely have faith to believe the gospel. They have no riches to trust in. The early church saw ministry to the poor as a vital part of the gospel (2 Cor. 8,9; Gal. 2:10). The church today needs to expand it's gospel vision and resources so that much of the dependence on social welfare by the poor, widows and orphans in the body of Christ is taken over by the church. This would, of course, require significant changes. Circumstances of the future will move the church in this direction.

6. The principle of *nourishment.*
Nations and cultures of the world are uniquely characterized by what their people eat. The kingdom of God is the one kingdom where the only food is the King himself.

> *Since there is ONE bread, we who are many are one body; for we all partake of the one bread.* (1 Cor. 10:17)

This principle is taught in John's gospel (John 6:26-63). Food becomes nourishment to our bodies through two actions: ingestion and digestion. if one's intestines and related organs cannot digest food that is eaten, it will not provide nourishment and the body will grow weak. There are also two processes in spiritual nourishment; these are revelation and obedience. Jesus stated that His words are spirit and they are life. First, they must be *spiritually* revealed to our hearts as truth. Then if we obey them, they become *life* within us and we are strengthened in Him.

Jesus told His disciples that He had food to eat they did not know about. That food was *to do* the will of His Father, and to accomplish His work (Jn. 4:32-34). Jesus then pointed to the fields, already white for harvest, as the Father's work. Those who only rejoice in revelation will not have sufficient strength in Christ to minister the gospel of the kingdom. The ones who hear, and who also delight to obey what is revealed to them, will receive nourishment and spiritual strength. The issue for Christians is not a question of success or failure but of obedience or disobedience (1 Jn. 2:5-6). Increase in godliness comes from obedience, which introduces the next principle.

7. The principle of *increase*.

Developed nations of the world fall into one of two classes: socialism or capitalism. Socialism teaches, "take from the one who has and give to the one who does not have." The kingdom of God teaches, "take from the one who does not have, and give to the one who has." Capitalism teaches, "invest and save, and you will acquire gain." The kingdom of God teaches, "diligently use and give away your resources, and they will increase." The kingdom of God is not a righteous expression of socialism any more than it is a righteous expression of capitalistic democracy.

The following verses of scripture express the principle of increase that is unique to the kingdom of God.

> *Give, and it shall be given to you again; good measure, pressed down, shaken together, running over, they will pour into your lap. For by YOUR standard of measure it will be measured to you again.* (Lk. 6:38)

> *There is one who scatters, yet increases all the*

> *more, and there is one who withholds what is due, but it results only in want.* (Pr. 11:24-25)

This principle applies to *all* spiritual resources, not just to money given to the Lord's work. For example, a pastor to whom the Lord has given authority to oversee a church has an option; he can exercise this authority and keep it to himself, or he can train and raise up responsible men of character to whom he delegates some responsibility. By doing so, he shares his authority. Over time, the original authority given by the Lord will increase in these men as they mature and prove themselves in their ministries. In time, they will delegate some of their authority to other men they have trained. And so as authority is delegated it continues to grow, and men are trained, something that must occur if the church is to be restored to the apostolic pattern of the New Testament.

In the first instance where authority was not delegated, that church would eventually reach a level where it would simply strive to maintain itself. Although there might be increase in numbers, it would *not* produce spiritual fathers, men committed to train other men with a vision of seeing greater stature in their "sons" than they themselves have in Christ.

One consequence of an environment where believers are free to exercise spiritual gifts and ministries, is that in doing so, they encourage other members to participate. Thus, various giftings of the Spirit multiply in an assembly the more they are used. In addition, each individual ministry grows in depth and quality the more it is used in service. For example, one who is faithful in prayer will develop a more effective prayer life over time. This is how intercessors are born!

The principle of increase is essential to *every* application of ministry of the gospel. Indeed, it was the very first principle ever manifested when God offered up His son in order to gain many more sons for Himself. It was first demonstrated by God's people when Abraham paid tithes to the Lord in the person of Melchizedek (Gen. 14:18-20). For believers, or churches, to ignore this principle is to open themselves to the curse of poverty (Mal. 3:8-11).

To be God's witness in the days of darkness ahead a church must be richly endowed with spiritual gifts, ministries, power evangelism, servant-leaders, godly character, family order, prayer and a vision for the day in which they are living. A key to attaining these things is commitment to the principles of increase. Where apostolic churches exist, they have a responsibility to exercise this principle by in releasing translocal ministries to build and strengthen other bodies of believers. Ministries are not given to individual assemblies; they are intended for the whole body of Christ. thus, there must be a willingness to release such men to travel as the Lord leads. The ultimate application of this principle in the life of a believer occurs, when of his own free will, he offers up himself as a bond-servant for the service to which he has been called. This leads us to the next principle.

8. The principle of *stature.*

Nations of the world give titles and offices to honor great ones of their lands. Stature in God's kingdom is a matter of character. Stature is not simply a matter of avoiding sin; it is *how great one is in the eyes of the Lord* (Lk. 1:15). We tend to measure spiritual stature by the fruit we see in ministry. However, God measures it by obedience and humility (1 Cor. 1:26-29). It is worth noting that He is committed to destroy the pride and loftiness of man (Is. 2:11-22). While stature is not a measure of excellence in performance, it is a measure of relationship between character and responsibility in one's service. The following verses define spiritual stature.

> *Blessed are the poor in spirit, for theirs is the kingdom of God.* (Mt. 5:3)
>
> *Blessed are the meek (humble) for they shall inherit the earth.* (Mt. 5:5)
>
> *Whoever then humbles himself as this child, he is the greatest in the kingdom of heaven.* (Mt. 18:4)

The preceding principles of the kingdom have been ordered in their presentation since each one is built on those that came before it. This eighth principle is key in qualifying leaders of the church (1 Tim. 3:1-10). Stature is what makes bond-servants; and above all else leaders are to be bond-servants. Jesus made this abundantly clear in the example of His own life. He also made it clear in His charge to the early apostles (Mt. 20:25-28).

It is significant that when Jesus identified Himself as the One who will shepherd His church and guide them to springs of living waters He used the (GRK) word "ARNION" meaning "a little lamb" to express His stature as leader (Rev. 7:17). Jesus was faithful as a lamb when shepherded by His Father; this was what qualified Him to be our Shepherd. In the same way, unless leaders are willing to be shepherded, they will not have the stature to shepherd others. The following verse is our Lord's invitation to develop stature.

> *Take My yoke upon you and learn of Me, for I am gentle and humble of heart; and you will find rest for your souls.* (Mt. 11:29)

When we are lowly in our own eyes, it is easy to work with other believers; which brings us to the last principle.

9. The principle of *unity.*

> *And if a kingdom is divided against itself, that kingdom can not stand.* (Mk. 3:24)
>
> *... conduct yourselves in a manner worthy of the gospel of Christ ... that you are standing firm in ONE spirit, with ONE mind, STRIVING TOGETHER for the faith of the gospel.* (Phil. 1:27)

This ninth principle is essential to bring a fullness of gospel witness to the nations. When the purpose of God for the church is completed, all living stones who have a place in His house will have been gathered in; the church will stand triumphant as "one new man" in the earth exhibiting the fullness of Christ. How do we come to such a place of unity in the faith? The division that exists today among God's people discredits our words of witness for Christ. The thrust of teaching on this subject is often very superficial. Unity is generally equated to being in agreement on doctrine and practice. In fact, Christians are one *in identity* because they bear His name, and they are one *in essence* because they share His life, and they are one *in practice* to the extent that they put on His character. Thus, unity is *altogether* a question of our relationship to Jesus. There is hope for unity when we can submit to others in our diversity.

> *... Holy Father, keep them in Thy name, THE NAME WHICH THOU HAST GIVEN ME, THAT THEY MAY BE ONE, even as we are.* (Jn. 17:11)

It is quite clear that the essence of being in the body of Christ is a work of the Holy Spirit:

> *For by ONE SPIRIT we were ALL baptized into ONE BODY ... and we were ALL made to drink of ONE SPIRIT.* (1 Cor. 12:13)

It is not so obvious how we are perfected in unity by the glory of God.

> *And the GLORY which Thou has given me I have given to them; THAT THEY MAY BE ONE, just as We are one; I IN THEM, and Thou in Me, THAT THEY MAY BE PERFECTED IN UNITY ...* (Jn. 17:22-23)

How can glory be the basis of unity? When Moses asked God to show His glory to him, the Lord responded by declaring His name and His goodness (or character) to Moses (Ex. 33:18-19; 34:6-7). Thus, in this life God equates His glory to His nature (or character). In the spirit world, His glory would be a shekinah brightness that we could not behold in our flesh.

This relationship between character and glory was confirmed in the life of Jesus, for the disciples referred to His character by saying that they had beheld *His glory,* the glory of the only begotten of the Father, *full of grace and truth* (Jn. 1:14; Heb. 1:3). It is His nature (or glory) revealed in our lives, not our understanding of Him, that draws men to Jesus and promotes unity in the body of Christ. This is quite apparent in scriptures such as Eph. 4:1-3 and Col. 3:12-15, which exhort us to put on kindness, humility, patience, forbearance, forgiveness, etc. as the means of becoming, in practice, the one body we are called to be in Christ. Love is defined as the *perfect bond of unity.* The proof of our identity to the world depends on the reality of our love for one another.

> *By this ALL MEN will know that you are My disciples, if you have love for one another.* (Jn. 13:35)

The first step toward unity is to recognize what has divided the body of Christ over the years, to repent and then turn away from such practices. Whenever man has usurped control from the Holy Spirit in the church, exclusivity has been birthed around issues such as organization, ministry emphasis, and legalistic applications of scriptures to define behavior. Important as they are, such things as correct doctrine, miracles of healing and deliverance, etc., can never alone bring unity. Unity is not a question of conformity, but of being one in mind, speech and judgement despite diversity; with each believer serving in brokenness out of the burden God has placed in his heart. We must continually guard against spirits of elitism, competition or divisiveness. Hardship and many other diverse pressures from unpleasant events in the days ahead will serve to promote unity. Historically, persecution produces purification and unites believers around the One they love. The crucible of spiritual warfare the church will face in the days ahead requires the disciplined unity of an army (Joel 2:7-11). Only the Lord would use military techniques and warfare to prepare His bride! A healthy body and a well trained army both express the unity between component parts that the Lord is going to bring forth in His Church. What was once a scattered pile of dry bones will one day have the witness of a mighty army!

> *So I prophesied as He commanded me, and ... the bones came together, bone to it's bone ...*

> *and sinews covered them, and flesh grew and skin covered them ... and breath came into them, and they came to life, and stood on their feet, an EXCEEDINGLY GREAT ARMY.* (Ez. 37:7-10)

Demons from the gates of hell who are powers behind the New Age movement and agents of Satan's strategy to deceive mankind into taking the mark of the beast will *not* prevail against the church. She will be a fortress or ark of safety in that day!

The world has yet to see the full witness of the Lord's gospel in the church. This is surely to come to pass in the days ahead as these nine principles are manifest in the lives and message of those preaching the gospel of the kingdom.

THE CHURCH AND THE KINGDOM

The gospel of the kingdom being the message of the church raises the following question, "What is the relationship of the church to the kingdom of God, and how are they distinct from one another?" The following five truisms serve to answer this question:

1. God's kingdom exists wherever He reigns. Thus, the kingdom of heaven is also the kingdom of God. When the Lord's prayer, "Thy kingdom come, Thy will be done on earth as it is in heaven" is answered, the "kingdom of earth" will also be the kingdom of God. Indeed, bringing this to pass is His purpose in this particular period of the church age.
2. The kingdom of God has always existed. It has no beginning and no end for it represents the sphere of God's dominion. On the other hand, the church began on the day of Pentecost.
3. The kingdom is perfect since God and His government are perfect. The kingdom is not being built, it is being extended as men submit to His government. In contrast, the church today is imperfect, but she is

growing into a future perfect maturity as she is being built by the Lord. This perfection is centered in the purpose of God.

4. The gospel is the gospel of the kingdom, not of the church; the church is the instrument of God to minister the gospel. The church's commission is to bring about, through spiritual ministry and warfare, the reality and fulfillment of the Lord's victory at Calvary in the lives of all who believe the gospel.
5. The present ministry of the church will continue until *all* enemies are under His feet, and the Lord Jesus has come to have *first place in everything* (Col. 1:18; Heb. 10:12-13). At that time, the bride of Christ will have made herself ready and God will then come and dwell among His people in the holy city, the new Jerusalem, His chosen place of rest (Rev. 21:1-3). Thus, the future center of the kingdom, the Zion of God from where His government will go forth over all creation, will be an overcoming company who have been conformed into the image of Jesus (Ro. 8:14-19, 29-30; 2 Tim. 2:11-12; Rev. 2:26-27; 3:12, 21; 20:4-6; 21:7; 22:3-5). All of creation is eagerly awaiting this unveiling of the sons of God; a climactic consequence of the gospel of the kingdom.

THE END TIME WITNESS OF THE GOSPEL

The twenty-fourth chapter of Matthew's gospel reveals that the church today stands at a unique period of time in the purpose of God. In this particular scripture, His disciples asked Jesus a crucial question:

> *... Tell us ... what will be the sign of Your coming and the end of the age?* (Mt. 24:3)

In answer, Jesus described many aspects of tribulation that would come to pass first, and which would intensify just prior to His return. These included wars, famines, earthquakes, persecutions, great deception and cosmic disturbances. *[11,14] Such happenings are always relative. Christians living in Germany during the end of World War II probably believed that was the end; the same could be said for Christians in Russia or China under the communists. However, *one thing above all else,* would clearly point to His return and the end of the age! Furthermore, it was a sign that the church would be able to recognize.

> *And this GOSPEL OF THE KINGDOM shall be preached in the whole world FOR A WITNESS TO ALL THE NATIONS, and then the end shall come.* (Mt. 24:14)

The days that lie ahead are not only a time of tribulation, but also glorious days of church restoration and a great ingathering of souls as the gospel of the kingdom becomes a distinct witness to all nations. This is more than the ministry of evangelism, for God's strategy is not to gather a great harvest without preparing "His barns" to receive it.

A restored church is beginning to emerge in the earth. Bonds that have held the church to techniques and methods of the world and to religious traditions are being broken. The Lord is raising up a new generation of bond-servants upon whom He will write the gospel of the kingdom for this generation to read, a gospel unique in its power of witness.

Jesus did not come to earth simply to give us His words; He came to give us Himself. Therefore, to minister the gospel is to minister "the Lord of the word," not just "the word of the Lord." The gospel of the kingdom is not simply words, it is a demonstration of the power and character of God.

* 11: pp 259-272

> *For the kingdom of God does not consist in words but IN POWER.* (1 Cor. 4:20)

It is not a definition of religious conduct; it is the righteousness of God expressed in lives; how we love one another; how we walk in victory standing against the works of darkness around us; and how we reflect compassion for the lost.

> *For the kingdom of God is not eating and drinking, but RIGHTEOUSNESS and PEACE and JOY in the Holy Spirit.* (Ro. 14:17)

It is a time of transition. [15] We are entering a new era in the history of the church, one which is intricately woven into God's purpose for this age. All is on schedule! When the Lord initiated His redemptive plan for mankind, He foreknew all things, and where we are today is *exactly* where He knew we would be. Nothing has occurred that was not foreknown. At no time has the Lord ever reacted to unexpected circumstances. All is in His hands. We who are alive in Christ today were also foreknown; thus, it is not by accident we have been called into His purpose now and not in some previous generation. We have been brought to the kingdom for just such a time as this!

Many Christians are simply waiting for the Lord to come and rapture them out of the calamities they see coming upon the earth. This is a very selfish mind-set which misses entirely what is in the Lord's heart. He is coming for a bride who has prepared and given herself to His purpose in these days. It is not a time to fly away and escape but a time to overcome. It is a day to do battle for the souls of men against the world forces of darkness and spiritual authorities in heavenly places.

The very darkness and difficulties that men seek to escape from are events intended by God to bring the church to maturity and prepare her for a great end time ministry. Unsaved men will be brought to a place of decision when they see that the arm of flesh does not have the answers. As a consequence, there will be a great ingathering of souls.

There will also be a falling away. Some with shallow roots will grow cold and apathetic because of conditions and fall away; others will fall prey to deceiving spirits of the occult (Mt. 24:9-12; 1 Tim. 4:1-3).

Much ministry has historically contained a mixture of God's anointing and the arm of flesh. There will be no such mixture in that which is to come; God will move in such a sovereign way all will know that His Spirit is doing the work, and the Lord shall be glorified!

The lack of character God has tolerated in ministers of the past will not be allowed in these days; we shall again see a reverence for God that existed in the days of Ananias and Sapphira (Acts 5:3-11).

The Lord has promised to shake *all* things, including heaven and earth (Heb. 12:25-29; Hag. 2:6-9). Everything that can be shaken will be shaken, which includes what has been built by the arm of flesh in churches. The fire of God will test and reveal the quality of all that has been built or promoted in his name (1 Cor. 3:13). Many ministries will experience the smell of smoke as He touches works of the flesh such as hidden sins, pride, spirits of control and manipulation, etc. The soulish shall be separated from the spiritual; the holy from the profane.

These are days to learn more perfectly how to enter into His rest and cease from programs designed to make a church look successful in our eyes.

If we are committed to serve, we will be willing to make transitions. Transition in how we minister, how we relate together and how we build in the house of God; even the reason for ministry will change, for the purpose of God, not the needs of man, must undergird our service. Because all things concerning the end times have been foreknown by God, He has defined and is preparing the works that are necessary for His strategy to be completed.

I believe that the greatest demonstration of power in the history of the church lies just ahead as the gospel of the kingdom is demonstrated and preached to all nations. This requires the eyes of our hearts to be opened in faith to see what the Lord wishes to do; not only *what* He will do, but also the *magnitude* as well. However, faith alone is not sufficient; our hearts must be prepared in true lowliness and humility so that all glory will go to the Lord.

The Lord is mobilizing and preparing His army on earth; our confidence as soldiers is *not* in our abilities, but *in Him* and the strength of His might. Our responsibility is to be committed to our place of service so that we all stand and move as one man. One Lord, one body, one gospel!

The forces that God is mobilizing also include the elements and ecological factors of the world. Earthquakes, famines, hurricanes, droughts, volcanos, floods, scarcity of commodities, etc. are tools He will use to get men's attention. Such things are not to be seen by the church as enemies but as her allies in accomplishing His purpose. The battle ground is the souls of men. There will eventually be no undecided men, for all will be brought to a place of decision in those days. This is the Lord's battle strategy.

> *Multitudes, multitudes in the valley of decision! For the day of the Lord is near in the valley of decision.* (Joel 3:14)

One current example is God's present judgement of the permissive life-style of today's society by the

AIDES epidemic. The crises to arise will bring times of judgement and circumstances that call men to repentance.

> *And I will display wonders in the sky and on the earth, blood, fire and columns of smoke. The sun will be turned into darkness, and the moon into blood before the great and awesome day of the Lord comes. And it will come about that WHOEVER calls on the name of the Lord will be delivered ...* (Joel 2:30-32)

There will also be economic disasters. The "house of cards" that have been built by the accumulation of national, business and personal debts will collapse. A mandatory step for the days ahead is to be out of debt and ensure that personal tithes and offerings are part of one's commitment to the life of a local assembly.

Finally, we must be prepared to see God move to bring down barriers that hinder fellowship between churches. Just as the Lord will do mighty deeds through the power of His Spirit, so also will He move sovereignly to unite His people in the cause of evangelism. We need to have a responsive and expectant heart to see the Spirit of Christ begin to bring His people together in a common, united witness. The fields that we would reap from in those days are fields we must sow today in preparation; therefore, we must strive for unity.

If we understand these things, our primary concern should be, first, that we are ready ourselves; and second, that we begin to prepare others for the unprecedented days of testing that lie ahead. For this reason, let us next examine what it means to equip the saints for their place of service in the body of Christ.

CHAPTER 4

EQUIPPING THE CHURCH

And He gave some as APOSTLES, and some as PROPHETS, and some as EVANGELISTS, and some as PASTORS and TEACHERS, for the EQUIPPING of the saints for the work of service to the BUILDING up of the body of Christ; until we ALL attain to the UNITY OF THE FAITH, to a MATURE man, to the MEASURE OF THE STATURE WHICH BELONGS TO THE FULLNESS OF CHRIST ... NO LONGER to be tossed here and there ... but SPEAKING THE TRUTH IN LOVE, we are to GROW UP in ALL ASPECTS INTO HIM who is the head, even Christ, from whom the WHOLE BODY, being fitted and held together by that which EVERY JOINT supplies, according to the PROPER WORKING OF EACH INDIVIDUAL PART causes the GROWTH of the body for the BUILDING UP OF ITSELF IN LOVE. (Eph. 4:11-16)

Many traditional practices, organizational concepts and techniques of service will be found wanting and be burned up in the crucible of shaking that lies ahead.

Only what is relevant to the Holy Spirit's ministry will remain in the armory of the Lord. The clergy/laity mind-set and the role of strong, dominant, independent individuals will fade away as the body of Christ comes to maturity.

Nominal church membership will be replaced by deep personal commitments to the Lord.

The measure of success by head count in a church will be replaced by the quality of spiritual life that is present. There may well be large churches, but it will be the power and presence of Jesus that marks their success.

Not all believers will make these transitions but those who are equipped by the Spirit will do so.

THE THREE COMMISSIONS

There are three great commissions contained in scripture that pertain to the church. The first is one assumed by the Lord, which assures the church of her final triumph and is the basis of the other two commissions.

> ... *And upon this rock (confession that Jesus is the Christ, the Son of God) I WILL BUILD MY CHURCH; and the gates Hades shall not overpower it.* (Mt. 16:18)

It is certain that all labor in vain who choose to build in His church independent of Him or contrary to His ways (Ps. 127:1). His strategy is perfect, and this guarantees the final, glorious consummation of His purpose for the church.

The second commission is familiar to every believer, for it is the command to the church to go into all the world and preach the gospel to every creature. This commission began at the Lord's ascension; and when it is completed the Lord will return. The gospel is more than an invitation to accept Jesus as one's Savior; it is the gospel of His kingdom.

Go into all the world and PREACH THE GOSPEL TO ALL CREATION. (Mk. 16:15)

The third commission is expressed in Eph. 4:11-13. It concerns the responsibility and grace that five specific ministries have been given to equip the saints for their work of service in the body of Christ, which *includes preaching the gospel of the kingdom.* It is apparent from this scripture, that without apostles and prophets, saints cannot be fully equipped for their work of service. However, by the same reasoning, once these ministries are restored, there then exists the full potential of seeing the Lord's body equipped for service, and the church coming into the maturity that belongs to the fullness of Christ. Thus, this third commission, within the context of Eph. 4:12-16, would seem to represent what is yet lacking in church restoration.

WHAT IT MEANS TO EQUIP A BELIEVER

The word "equipping" is translated from the Greek word "KATARTISMOS," which comes from two root words, "KATA" meaning "according to," and "ARTIOS" meaning "complete." Several other translations of the Bible use the words, "Perfecting" or "completing." The thought communicated implies a *total readiness* within the context of what one is called *to be* and *to do.*

There are three essential areas in which believers are equipped for their work of service in the body of Christ.

1. Godly character
2. As a priest (prayer and worship)
3. Vocational gifts and ministries

To the same extent that any of these areas are neglected, or deficient, one's service will also fall short. It should be noted that gifts and ministries are transient, being confined to this life, while the other two are eternal. Therefore, they are the most important areas to be addressed in the equipping process.

GETTING RID OF IDOLS

God hates idolatry and wants us to flee from it, and to guard ourselves from idols (1 Cor. 10:14; I Jn. 5:21).

I am sure most Christians view idolatry as a sin largely confined to pagan lands with very little relevance to our nation. However, such is not the case. Whatever takes first place, *ahead of the Lord,* in the desires and affections of one's heart *is an idol.*

God created man for Himself, with an inner hunger for and capacity to worship Him. When we do not put Him first, we will focus our inner affection on something or someone else.

Satan also recognizes these idols, and his demons work to draw men and women further into an obsession and worship of them. An idol has no power by itself alone, but because they provide access for demons they are most destructive (1 Cor. 8:4-6; 1 Cor. 10:19-20).

One can group idols into roughly four classes.

1. Idols made out of wood, stone, etc. (Deut. 4:23-28).
2. Living creatures (e.g., Hindu worship of snakes; worship of men such as Father Divine, Mohammed, etc.).
3. Possessions and lusts of one's heart. Greed is equivalent to idolatry (Col. 3:5). Money, a car or a house can be idols.
4. "Christian" idols. One can so follow a prominent ministry, a denomination or a theological emphasis to the extent that they displace the Lord in one's heart. Also, a minister can worship the success and dimensions of his own ministry more than the Lord.

Idols of these last two classes are present in the church today and must *first* be forsaken before one can be equipped for service in the house of God.

WHO DOES THE EQUIPPING?

Scripture is clear that elders of a local assembly are *solely* responsible in the Lord to shepherd and feed the flock of God entrusted to their oversight (Acts 14:23; 20:17,28; 1 Pet. 5:1-3). It is equally clear from scripture that the Lord has deposited grace and anointing in the five ministries of Eph. 4:11 to equip the saints. In order to reconcile those two assignments, it is apparent that elders *must be men graced with one of the five ministry gifts.* To simply be a good administrator does not qualify one for eldership. Since men must also satisfy requirements in character, home order, experience and secular life to qualify as elders, there can be men in the assembly whose anointing makes it clear they have a call to one of the five ministries, but who cannot yet meet all the requirements for eldership. Such men could be used in the equipping process under the supervision of the elders. Home group leadership is a possible example of their service. Indeed, every active member of a body can contribute to the equipping of others through prayer, spiritual gifts and ministries of relationship.

The mantle of responsibility to ensure that a necessary diversity exists, as needed, to equip the saints rests upon the elders. This becomes a much easier task once there are other assemblies in a region with whom ministries can be exchanged; and especially when apostolic and prophetic ministries are available to strengthen churches.

The local church is God's seminary. A seminary by definition, is "an environment in which something originates and from which it is propagated." Everything which the Lord has created with life is able to reproduce itself; a local expression of the body of Christ is no exception. Although evangelistic ministries may be involved, apostolic and prophetic ministries are *necessary* to lay the foundation for a true New Testament expression of the body of Christ (Eph. 2:20-22). Developing this fathering aspect of church reproduction is part of the equipping task.

In a very general sense, one can express the purpose of each of the five fold ministries as follows:

1. In their *burden,* the Lord wants His people to be *evangelistic* so that the gospel will always be proclaimed.
2. In their *knowledge,* He wants His people to be *teachers* so that they can instruct one another in His ways.
3. In their *heart,* He wants His people to be *pastoral* so that they will love and care for one another.
4. In their lives, He wants His people to be *prophetic* so that *how* they live and *what* they minister expresses the "now" word of the Lord.
5. In their *vision,* He wants His people to be apostolic so that they will always minister out of His purpose. Vision includes both foresight and insight; foresight into *what* God purposes to do, and insight into *how* to move with Him.

EQUIPPED IN DIVERSITY

> *For since the creation of the world His invisible attributes, His eternal power and divine nature have been clearly seen, being understood through what has been made.* (Ro. 1:20)

There is no question about God's power when one considers the immensity of creation. However, it is not so obvious what there is in creation that points to His invisible attributes and divine nature. One such attribute is "order" and another is "diversity". Let us consider the latter.

When one beholds a beautiful flower he is stirred by the creative ability of God. However, it is only in the sum total of all flower species, each one with it's unique coloring, scent, shape, eco-system and other physical characteristics that we begin to grasp the magnificent beauty of floral creation.

If we do some bird watching and listen to the various songs we again appreciate the great diversity there is in the many songs and plumage of bird life. Again, it is the integrated total beauty of all birds that express God's creative genius.

When we consider the heavenly bodies God has placed in space, we see the same attribute of diversity manifest by the variety of planets, stars, constellations, quasars, etc. where there exists great differences in luminosity, mass, location, orbit and composition. Truly, the heavens declare the glory of God!

If we examine the diverse crystalline structures in precious stones we discover that a unique order and arrangement of the atoms determines the brilliance and color of each jewel.

One can conclude from these observations that God's heart was never to create clones, but to demonstrate the grandeur and glory of His divine nature through a spectacular diversity of beauty and function in each created specie. And this truth is a fundamental guiding principle in equipping believers for their place of service.

The body of Christ is to function just as a healthy physical body would. This means that each member is equipped for a unique place of service, and when all members are so functioning in their diversity, the church becomes as "one great man" moving under the headship of Christ.

There are essentially four phases in the equipping process: manhood, priesthood, servanthood and fatherhood. It was stated earlier that one is equipped in three areas: in character (i.e., manhood), as a priest (priesthood) and in vocational giftings (servanthood). One objective of being equipped is to be able to impart to others what God has built in us. This reproduction in others is what fatherhood relates to.

Let us now examine each of these four aspects of being equipped to better understand what is involved.

1. Manhood

God has revealed in scripture that He seeks to have a family of sons (Ro. 8:14-19). All sons will bear the image of Christ, but each one will be unique and diverse as they appear before Him. Why would God want a family of clones? Would we want each of our children to look and speak exactly alike? We will all bear the image of the heavenly Father because we each have His nature within us. However, there will be specific characteristics, degrees of glory as well as levels of responsibility that will make each of us unique in the kingdom to come. God's work in creation points to this desire for His family.

The place we are called to fill in His purpose during our generation, and subsequently the future role we will play in His family of sons, were in the heart of God when He formed us in our mother's womb. Fore-knowing our response to the gospel, our failures, the circumstances we would face, the spouse we would have and the dimensions of our sphere of service, He has alloted grace to us and placed within certain qualities that will enable us to perform the work of service He has prepared for us. Within us there are diverse latent abilities and characteristics that make each of us a unique person, and when anointed by the Holy Spirit they constitute a unique expression of service in the body of Christ.

None of these properties have any value in the kingdom until they have been laid down in death at the cross. When we have wholeheartedly done so, God can raise them up and sanctify them for His use. We can then be equipped for service. There is sufficient grace for each one of us!

It is good to remember that only one Son, Jesus, will possess *all* the fullness of God, be the *exact* representation of His nature and be the full radiance of His glory. The potential for this to be expressed in personality, appearance, wisdom, emotions, and speech in a Man was prepared in the Holy Embryo within the womb of Mary (Is. 49:1-9).

The qualities that Jeremiah required to be a prophet to nations were created in him and consecrated by God while he was yet in his mother's womb.

> *Before I formed you in the womb I knew you (i.e., all about you), and before you were born I consecrated you; I have appointed you a prophet to the nations.* (Jer. 1:5)

Inherent in God's call was His foreknowledge of Jeremiah's training as a child, his family, and secular life as well as his obedience to God's call on his life.

Paul was prepared for service as a man while in his mother's womb, and when separated from her by birth was called to reveal the Lord Jesus; a call he embraced in adulthood after years of preparation in Jewish culture (Gal. 1:16-17). It was no accident that his voice was contemptible.

David appeared to understand clearly how he, too, was prepared in the womb of his mother to serve the purpose of God in his generation.

> *For Thou didst form my inward parts (personality, capacity to express God, etc.) Thou didst weave me (all the properties of his person) in my mother's womb. I will give thanks to Thee for I am fearfully and wonderfully made; wonderful are Thy works, and my soul (my mind, intellect, memory, will) knows it very well. My frame (physical stature) was not hidden from Thee, when I was made in secret, and skillfully wrought in the depths of the earth. Thine eyes have seen my unformed substance (from developing embryo to complete man); and in Thy book they were all written, the days that were ordained for me, when as yet there was not one of them.* (Ps. 139:13-16)

The following is a list of the major parameters whose derivatives together make a person unique and diverse from others.

1. Personality. Different personalities are expressed in terms of certain behaviorial temperaments, each of which is a unique grouping of personal traits pointing to specific strengths and weaknesses, (i.e., friendly, talkative, unstable, decisive, etc.)
2. Intelligence and physical abilities (or limitations).
3. Capacity to express God's life (i.e., the songs of Fanny Crosby, the writings of Jamie Buckingham, the acts of mercy by Mother Theresa, etc.)
4. Family life. (Parents and spouse).
5. Sex, race and ethnic background.
6. Culture (education and social training).
7. Secular life (trade, profession, occupation).
8. Community life (ghetto, farm, middle class, etc.).

The Lord sees each of His children as uniquely diverse but of equal worth; as distinct but without partiality in His eyes (Gal. 3:28). We all have the same call: to lay down our lives in total commitment to Jesus, knowing that apart from Him we can do nothing or be of no value in His kingdom. Even before we responded to His call He foreknew the mistakes and disasters we would make from going our own way. Even these were used by the Lord to prepare us for service.

Our equipping can *only* begin after we come to a place of commitment. At that time the cross is key. All of our manhood (or womanhood) must embrace death at the cross if it is to be raised up anointed and equipped for service. The cross is how the Lord can anoint a poor illiterate handicapped person to bring glory to Him. Although there are not many, it is also how He can use a a wealthy, highly talented individual.

What we have been through in the past can contribute to our preparation for serving Him. Therefore, we should *not* keep looking back and regretting past mistakes. The Lord knew that we would do so and has provided grace accordingly. Our mistakes and sins are under His blood. We are to focus on His call for our life today and on the grace that is ours for what lies ahead.

2. Priesthood

There is no greater realm of service than being a priest of the Lord in worship, thanksgiving, prayer and intercession. Just as manhood marks one's identification in the human realm, so priesthood is where we develop and strengthen our spiritual union with God as a son. His presence is the place of revelation where we discover our call and understand the purpose of God; where we learn of the Lord's burdens and strategies, and where we receive the grace we will need to respond. This is where we more fully come to know Him. The ultimate goal of being equipped as a priest is to know Him and His ways well enough to enter into His rest. Just as the cross was key in manhood, so also *His rest* is key in priesthood.

Music has become an increasingly important voice for the youth culture of the world. The progression seen over the years in country music, rock and hard rock are examples of this cultural expression. Satan has used such music to present his spirit and message of rebellion to entice young people to himself.

As increasing numbers of the youth are saved and come into the church they bring with them a desire to use their music to serve the Lord. However, such talent has no place in the kingdom simply because the words and tunes have been reformed.

Both motivation and abilities must first be laid down to experience death at the cross. Then the Lord can resurrect *whatever* He wishes, and do so *whenever* He desires.

All believers are priests before God. However, the Lord is going to raise up many from among the youth of today with a special priesthood ministry. With voices, instruments and dances they will minister the song of the Lord to Him. Their ministry will be a special source of strength in times of spiritual warfare.

As order is restored to the house of God so also will there be a mighty restoration in spiritual worship. This ministry will be a key for believers being able to reign in the midst of their enemies, trials, circumstances and crises (1 Chron. 25).

> ... *for the joy of the Lord is your strength.* (Neh. 8:10)

3. Servanthood

Corresponding to the cross and spiritual rest, the key in ministry is *servanthood.* What one is equipped for in ministry will have little value to others unless it comes from a servant's heart. Ministry is not primarily an act of "doing something", it is an impartation of life. Ministry does not originate in one's office, position or abilities, it comes from the heart of God. Therefore, true ministry will *always* glorify Christ.

In this dimension of equipping, the Lord completes the diversity He has planned before the world began for His body. Although there are nine spiritual gifts (1 Cor. 12:8-10), there are many other giftings of the Spirit prepared for the saints such as helps, hospitality, showing comfort, etc.

> *Now there are VARIETIES of gifts, but the same Spirit. There are VARIETIES of ministries but the same Lord. And there are VARIETIES of effects, but the same God who works ALL THINGS in ALL PERSONS.* (1 Cor. 12:4-6)

The magnitude of diversity available to the body of Christ when it is fully equipped can be grasped by multiplying the array of spiritual gifts and ministries by the array of manhood parameters. Combinations are blended together for each believer according to God's call and grace extended to that person.

Thus God equips us with unique diverse qualities so that in our service He is able to use them to work varieties of effects in the lives of others. What God has given to each one is exactly what will be needed to redeem and bring certain others into the kingdom and His purpose. Consider for a moment how the Lord would equip men to evangelize and plant churches among the militant Moslems of Iran or the Aborigines in the Australian out-back. This could only be done through lives that were uniquely prepared by God to preach the gospel of the kingdom effectively in those cultures.

It is God who places us where He desires in His body both functionally and geographically, and it is God who determines what our gifts and ministries are (1 Cor. 12:11,18).

Foreknowing our response to the gospel, and how past and future difficulties, mistakes, and circumstances will prepare us for service, He equips each member of His body for the work to which He has called them.

5. Fatherhood

As the process of church restoration continues we will see men equipped for service who excel their fathers in excellence of ministry and eventually in stature. Just as there was a declension of quality during the first century of the church, so now there will be an ascension in quality as the church is built and prepared for His return. This aspect of restoration is what Jesus referred to in His statement that, "Elijah is to come and restore all things" (Mt. 17:10). Elijah spent ten years as a spiritual father equipping Elisha to carry on his ministry as prophet (1 Kings 19; 2 Kings 2). The greater excellence in Elisha's ministry and character, when compared to Elijah (no self pity or fear of Jezebel), portray this principle of restoration. The church today needs the "spirit of Elijah"! The spirit of fatherhood that rested upon Elijah is essential today to turn the hearts of fathers toward equipping spiritual sons for service (Mal. 4:5-6).

The ultimate fruit of being equipped for service is realized when one is able to impart into others what God has built into him (2 Tim. 2:2). Disciples do *not* have to make the same mistakes that their teachers did. And what is true of individuals is also true for churches! There should be an ever increasing excellence in the quality and soundness of local expressions of the body of Christ as the church is restored.

Consider the following scenario. A man of God emerges in an area with a strong charismatic anointing resting upon his ministry, so that many are drawn to the Lord and around him. Because of the grace of God upon him, over time, a significant church develops with new believers continuing to gather around the man's ministry and under his leadership. He sets direction for and oversees the ever growing church. The fruits of ministry and a good character are evident throughout his lifetime. At his death, the mantle of leadership is passed on to the person who is considered most capable of carrying on his ministry.

This might appear to be a scenario of great success because of the multitude who were ministered to. However, this is not the case, for it is a picture of ministry without fatherhood. One can pass *nothing* of the Spirit on in death; this can only be done while we are alive! That is what fatherhood is all about. If the man in question had been committed to building and imparting into other men what God had given to him, he could have raised up many sons. Some would surely have exceeded him in ministry excellence and stature. Then at his death, there would have been no thought of looking for a successor. And in the end, many more would have been ministered to and no one person would be overly dominant.

EQUIPPED AS ONE BODY

By the nature of our humanity, unless we are restrained, we will go our own way. There is a discipline we must embrace if we want to walk united as one man with other believers. Jesus, Himself, underwent severe discipline to provide unity and wholeness to His body.

The word "discipline" is defined as, "rules that govern one's conduct." The Lord Jesus embraced a most painful discipline in order to make all believers into *one new man,* under His headship.

It was necessary for Him to shed His blood in order that our sins might be forgiven. However, the Lord's great agony, humiliation and suffering accomplished *much more.* The emphasis of the following scripture dealing with His death also indicates His purpose to bring forth His disciples in a one *united* body of believers.

> *But now in Christ Jesus you who formerly were far off have been brought near BY THE BLOOD OF CHRIST. For HE HIMSELF IS OUR peace, who made both groups into ONE, and broke down the barrier of the dividing wall, by abolishing IN HIS FLESH the enmity which is the Law of commandments contained in ordinances, that IN HIMSELF He might make the two into ONE NEW MAN, thus establishing peace, and might reconcile them both IN ONE BODY to God THROUGH THE CROSS, by it having put to death the enmity.* (Eph. 2:13-16)

The phrase, "by the blood of Christ" is the *one* and *only* way for mankind to receive forgiveness of sins and be reconciled to God. The phrases, "in Himself," "in His flesh" and "through the cross" were a part of His discipline in which He paid the price for all transgressions inherent in the human nature that keep believers from being one body. These include sins such as religious bigotry, racism, social or national elitism, respect of persons, human traditions and dogmatic positions. Our worth in God is equal, whether we are Jew or Gentile, slave or free man, and male or female (Gal. 3:27-28). *Jesus paid the price to be the one Shepherd of one flock* (Jn. 10:16). This truth must be *well* established in the hearts of those being equipped, for the great work that the Lord will do at the end of this age can *only* take place through a people *united* in Him.

There is also a three-fold discipline that local elders must embrace to equip the saints for service as a local expression of the body of Christ.

1. First, there *must* be a commitment to diversity in the eldership. There is no way that traditional methods can be adequate; one man leadership, Bible schools and teaching orientation based on a clergy-laity distinction will *always* fall short. The capability of any one minister can *never* match the value of diversity resident in the Lord's investment of grace and anointing in His five-fold ministries. The first discipline of a leader thus lies in *humility* and a *willingness too lay down personal prominence* and walk together in collegiality with other men; diversity with submission. Not only different graces in ministry but also divers behavioral temperaments are vital ingredients in an eldership. Healthy stresses between men, such as task oriented leaders with those who are people oriented, or the outspoken optimist with the cautious introvert, are what God uses to build mutual dependence between peers.

Each believer has been created with a unique group of behavioral traits and emotions as well as a specific inner capacity for expressing the life of God. There are no spiritual twins! When we come to Christ, He changes our nature into harmony with His own, but these personal attributes remain distinct. An extrovert does not become an introvert, but his outgoing ways are sanctified.

If there was but one minister to equip all members of a congregation their equipping would certainly be limited. Thus, diversity in leadership is required to fully equip the saints. The Lord speaks of His people as "living stones." Stones vary in shape, color and size. The human mind-set is to build with bricks which stress conformity in ministry, dress, worship, techniques, etc., but God only builds His house with stones.

2. Secondly, elders are responsible to provide an environment suitable for equipping the people. The pulpit ministry in congregational meetings, although essential, is not sufficient. More than a proclamation of truth is required if that truth is to become a living reality in the lives of those who hear it. There is also need for the informal atmosphere of small group gatherings, where believers are committed to help one another "work out" and "put on" the truth they are taught in central meetings. The essential dynamics of these small groups are members encouraging, admonishing, loving and challenging one another in their pursuit of the Lord. It is also the place where members can begin to "practice" their ministries; and where mistakes can be made without embarrassment. The oversight of these groups is also a place of training. Men, who the elders believe have a call and potential for eldership, can be delegated authority to exercise an accountable oversight of the groups. The early church, while it evangelized in the synagogues, was largely built in homes (Acts 2:46-27; 5:42; Ro. 16:5; 1 Cor. 16:19; Col. 4:15; Phil. 1:2).

Thus, the elders face a discipline of not only preaching truth, but also being responsible to see that truth fleshed out in the lives and service of the saints. As this takes place, the diversity of gifts and service that the Lord builds into His people will begin to appear and the body of the Lord will be manifest.

3. Thirdly, there is one more discipline for elders to embrace if the people are to fulfill their call in Christ. They must be *examples* of all they teach. They *cannot*

lead people into truth unless they themselves walk in truth (Jn. 17:19).

> *Remember those who led you, who spoke the word of God to you; and considering the result of their conduct, imitate their faith.* (Heb. 13:7)

> *Therefore, I exhort the elders ... proving to be examples to the flock.* (1 Pet. 5:1-3)

> ... *In speech, conduct, love, faith and purity, show yourself an example of those who believe.* (1 Tim. 4:12)

> *For you yourselves know how you ought to follow our example ... in order to offer ourselves as a model for you, that you might follow our example.* (2 Thess. 3:7-9)

An example is always the best teacher!

Each member of a local assembly also faces a discipline to become bonded to other members and personally equipped for service in that unique place prepared for them in the church. There are six areas of commitment which make up this discipline.

1. Commitment to *one* local church and its eldership as a place to become rooted in the Lord.
2. Commitment to be faithful in a home church. Many saints, over the history of the church, have attained great stature in character and ministry without ever experiencing the training of small groups. However, the emphasis today is not to raise up a few great men and women in Christ, but to raise up a church where members are strongly bonded together in Christ.
3. A commitment to accept other members in the group. There will be no progress until participants can accept one another just as Christ has accepted them (Ro. 15:7). Personality traits, biases, traditions, etc.

must cease to be important so that family relationships can be developed in the Spirit.

4. A commitment to recognize one's need for other members in the local group. The reality of 1 Cor. 12:21-22 must come alive in each heart. We do need one another!

5. A recognition and acceptance of one's own personal call and place of service in the body. It should become apparent to each member that they wear a pair of spiritual shoes that fits no one else.

6. The last step only becomes viable once the preceding five have been taken. It is a willing commitment to become open, honest and vulnerable with others of the group in dialogue, personal interaction, body ministry, confrontation and counsel. This is the process by which spiritual joints, sinews and tendons are developed that bond members together in a family relationship. This process will include a number of "non-church" issues such as home order, family priorities, and secular employment.

The long-range goal of the above steps is to equip members to be led of the Spirit in their specific sphere of service, to be willing to serve, and to be accountable to others in the Lord for their service.

SPIRITUAL PRINCIPLES FOR EQUIPPING

The dynamics of making disciples and equipping them for service requires two distinct meeting environments; a large central gathering and small group meetings usually held in selected homes. Of course, there will also be unstructured "one on one" encounters for the purpose of counsel, prayer and encouragement. However, regardless of where training takes place, there are certain invariant principles of the Spirit which must be constantly emphasized to keep the process from becoming simply a transfer of information.

The following are nine of the more important principles; each one is shown with the Spirit's emphasis contrasted to what is usually seen as important.

1. *Revelation vs. education.*

Revelation is the language of the Spirit. All that has been hidden from man, has been hidden in order that it might be revealed to those who seek Him. All who are equipped must learn this language! (Is. 55:8-9; Ro. 16:25; Eph. 1:17-23). Education fills the mind with information; revelation brings living truth into the heart.

> *For nothing is hidden, except to be revealed; nor has anything been secret, but that it should come to light. If any man has ears to hear, let him hear.* (Mk. 4:22-23).

2. *Obedience vs. knowledge.*

To receive revelation of truth, and to not obey that truth is like one eating food which he cannot digest; it will accomplish nothing! There are many Christians whose only emphasis is seeking new truth. However, God seeks for obedience *above all else*. Knowledge by itself alone only brings pride (1 Cor. 8:1). To be equipped for service is to bring the imaginations and speculations of our thought life concerning what we would like to do, captive in order to obey Christ (2 Cor. 10:3-5; Lk. 6:47-48). Today, in particular, is a day calling for obedience in the church.

3. *"Who" vs. "how" and "why."*

The way of uninspired theology is to define service in terms of methods and techniques. If one knows *"how"* to do something, he will not feel it is necessary to seek God for help. His method then becomes the "defined means" for his particular service. Without the Lord's anointing the means becomes a rigid inflexible "monument" as to how things will be done. This, of course, only leads to death. The progression is: man - method - means - monument - mortuary!

When the unexpected occurs in one's service, the way of the flesh is to ask, "why did this happen?" The Lord wants to equip us to not ask "why", but *"who"!* We need to know whether the adversary is responsible, whether it was a consequence of our own actions or whether the Lord has acted. Thus, we need only to seek the Lord for answers. The way of the Spirit is *always* to seek Christ, not answers. He is the one who establishes our steps in His way. Christianity is first of all *a Person,* who also is the way; *it is never* a philosophy or religious method (Pr. 16:9; 20:24; Ro. 8:14; Heb. 12:2).

4. *The purpose of God vs. the needs of mankind.* Many ministry endeavors and church strategies arise out of sincere desires and soulish emotions to meet needs. While the intention and zeal are good, the motivation is wrong. The purpose of God was established before the world was created, and it is *invariant* and *eternal.* Furthermore, His purpose is based on His foreknowledge of *all* needs in *all* persons in *every* generation. Each believer has been called to serve God so that His purpose in that particular generation can be accomplished. The call of God to each one of us is *always* accompanied by sufficient grace for whatever service we are called to, as well as for whatever circumstance we we may face in our response. Why did Jesus minister in certain cities of Israel rather than others? Why did He heal only one person at the pool of Bethesda? Why did He not speak out against slavery, etc.? The answers to such questions are hidden in the purpose of His Father. Likewise, in the purpose of God there is a unique place of service defined for each one of us from the foundation of the world. To seek the Lord and find that place is our first step in service, and it is also how the Lord will meet the needs of others through us.

5. *Character vs. deeds.*

The way of our flesh is to evaluate success in service by counting numbers; Sunday School attendance, size of the membership role, the number of decisions for Christ, the number healed, etc. Quality, not quantity, is the way of the Spirit. In the end it will also yield the greatest quantity of fruit. What one *is in Christ,* determines the worth of what one *does for Christ.* We may not be equipped to build "large churches" or achieve numerical success, but we are equipped to accomplish those deeds prepared for us from the foundation of the world (Eph. 2:10). Key in doing this is learning to enter into His rest, to become more like Him and more yielded to Him (Heb. 4:10-11). It is His life in us, His anointing that does the work. It is *never* a waste of time to sit in His presence when we are busy in service. There is no greater work than becoming like Jesus.

6. *Diversity vs. conformity.*

One major reason for the many schisms in Christendom is the religious practice of conforming groups of believers into various distinct theological molds based on doctrine, ministry, conduct, government or vision. Whether the primary issue was governmental or an interpretation of scripture (i.e. Catholicism or Protestantism) the end result was the same, "establish our conformity regardless of how it divides the body of Christ." Such conformity is a work of human ecclesiology. The way of the Spirit is to guide saints to one standard: "be conformed to the image of Christ." Within that standard and under His headship, they are equipped to manifest the *great diversity* implicit in the body of Christ. The Lord is building His house with living *stones* of different shapes, sizes and colors (1 Pet. 2:4). There are *no bricks* in it!

Furthermore, this diversity *must not* be tainted by

exclusivity; for there is no elitism, competition or schism in the Godhead or in the kingdom of God. Therefore, such things should not exist in the body of Christ.

7. *The sovereignty of God vs. circumstances.*

The way of the flesh is to equate our capability for success in service to the circumstances we face. When they are formidable, we lose faith to move forward; or if we see no obstacles we rush forward in our own strength. One who is equipped in the Spirit recognizes that success does not depend upon circumstances whether bad or good; it depends upon our willing *obedience* and *recognition* that the sovereignty of God undergirds whatever He has called us to do. He who calls us is faithful and able to bring it to pass. If we don't obey, He will raise up someone who will! (I Thess. 5:24). The entire word of God rests upon His sovereignty, much like a great weight would be supported on a table with four legs. If any of the legs were weak, the table would collapse. The table surface corresponds to the sovereignty of God without which there would be no Bible. The four legs represent four *unchanging* characteristics of God and mankind; if any one of these were taken away or weakened, the sovereignty of God (and thus His word) would collapse. These four "legs" are:

- The character (love) of God.
- The foreknowledge of God.
- The grace of God.
- The free will of man.

It is these four attributes of God and man, not circumstances, that make it certain we *can* fulfill our call in service, for they express the Lord's blend of Himself and His body. If our will was not required, we would only be robots; our faith is expressed through our wills (Ja. 2:17). However, if the grace of God was missing we could neither be or do anything for Him.

The *whole* plan of God flows out of His character, expressed in the love He had for sinners by sending His own Son to die for them. Above all else, the cross expresses God's heart toward us. Because of His foreknowledge, we can be *absolutely* confident that God has never reacted to any unexpected event, and where the *church* is, and where *we* are today, is *precisely* where He knew we would be before the foundation of the world. Thus, our faith in service must be grounded in the sovereignty of God.

8. *Bond-servants vs. rulers.*

The Lord's plan for man is that he rule over all creation (Heb. 2:5-8). This is part of the inheritance of those who overcome and prepare for it. The church is where we are trained and made ready to rule with Christ. Our place of future authority depends upon how well we serve today (Lk. 19:12-26; 2 Tim. 2:12, Rev. 2:26-27; 3:12; 5:9-10; 20:4-6; 22:3-5). The way of the flesh is "rise up, take control and rule." The way of the Spirit is the way of brokenness, to put on the Lord's yoke of meekness and lowliness and learn to serve. The Spirit does not equip us to serve as slaves, for a slave serves because circumstances compel him to do so. He prepares us to become bond-servants, for they enter into servitude of their own free will (Ex. 21:5).

> *Have this attitude (of heart) in yourselves which was also in Christ Jesus; who although He existed in the form of God, did not regard equality with God a thing to be grasped, but EMPTIED HIMSELF, TAKING THE FORM OF A BOND-SERVANT, and being made in the likeness of men..He humbled Himself by becoming obedient to the point of death, even death on a cross. THEREFORE, ALSO GOD HIGHLY EXALTED HIM ...* (Phil. 2:5-9)

Leaders will only be successful in equipping saints to serve if they themselves are good examples of bond-servants. New Testament apostles spoke of themselves as bond-servants; this was so real to them that it was an integral part of the gospel they preached (2 Cor. 4:5). When leaders are not equipped in this area of character, they seek to "rule well" rather than to "serve well." If men cannot walk together in submission to each other and serve one another, the easy way out is to create levels of authority with accountability only in one direction; and thus, hierarchical government is born. This is a key issue today in restoration of the church, for *servanthood* is an *essential* requirement for those leaders who God is raising up to guide His people in the days ahead.

9. *Spiritual warfare vs. warfare in the flesh.*

There is a great deal of concern today in the church concerning such issues as abortion, humanism, the teaching of evolution, terrorism, etc. The way of the flesh is to spend much time and resources on lobbies, legislation, elections, demonstrations, etc., as the church's strategy of warfare. Such efforts are not wrong, and within limits should be pursued. However, the forces behind these ungodly trends are Satanic and can only be defeated by spiritual warfare. The church is to be a prophetic voice for God against such things; she is also to pray for their removal and be prepared to battle in the Spirit against them. She is opposed by an organized hierarchy of Satanic hosts, apparently structured in five levels [16] (Eph. 6:12). These are as follows:

- *Satan,* who sees himself as God of this world.
- *Beelzebul,* who ranks next to Satan. He and Satan are the *rulers, principalities* or *sovereigns* over all the forces of evil. Apparently Satan has

placed Beelzebul to correspond to archangels in God's kingdom.

- *Authorities,* who are fallen angels directed by Beelzebul. They are authorities of evil over areas such as cities or nation.
- *Spiritual forces of wickedness* in heavenly places. These are fallen angels who carry out missions of wickedness under direction of the authorities.
- *World forces of darkness.* These are demons; spirit beings who are confined to the earth. Under the direction of fallen angels they tempt, corrupt, seduce and afflict mankind with activities such as war, terrorism, the occult, false signs, depression, fears, false ministries, humanism, sickness, perversions, deceptions, etc.

A major part of equipping the saints concerns spiritual warfare. They must be able to discern between "works of the flesh" and demonic activity. They must also know how to put on the armor God has provided and to rely on His strength (Eph. 6:10-18). There must *never be any fear* of Satan when they confront him or his agents. Spiritual warfare is an *integral* and *vital* part of the gospel of the kingdom.

The above nine maxims are spiritual truths which need to be *reinforced constantly* in the hearts of the saints, lest they forget and lapse into their own ways. To be equipped is *not a one time experience;* it is a *continuing* process.

THE CENTRAL MEETING

Elders need to maintain a clear distinction between the ministry content of home churches and the central meeting. Home churches must *not* become miniature replicas of the central gathering. For example, teaching would not be a primary emphasis in home groups, and the laying on of hands for impartation and directive prophecy should be confined to the central meeting. In a limited sense, these two meeting environments are analogous to the lecture auditorium and laboratory at college. Students are taught the theoretical content of their particular course of study in the lecture room; they then proceed to the laboratory for assignments that demonstrate the truth of what they were taught. The following is a topical overview of the various classes of ministry an eldership is responsible to provide in the central meetings in order to equip the saints:

1. Foundational teaching.

This is the essential foundational truths that establish new converts in Christ and His finished work at Calvary. This teaching should be given to believers as *soon* as possible after their conversion.

2. The gospel of the kingdom.

The *only* gospel ever given to the church is the gospel of the kingdom. As we have seen, it is the basis of *all* ministry of the Spirit in a *three-fold* sense. First, it is the message of God's saving grace, including His love and compassion for the poor and oppressed in power evangelism; second, it is the message and commission for spiritual warfare; and third, it includes all ministry that establishes the order of God's government. Thus, ministry in the home that brings godly order to pass is an expression of the gospel of the kingdom. It is the message that establishes the oversight of Christ in a church, and it is the message that will bring *all* enemies under the Lord's feet so that He comes to have *first* place in *everything.* It is also an everlasting gospel (Rev. 14:6). Thus, this gospel encompasses more than the salvation of lost men and the destruction of Satan's works; it is also the gospel of the glory of Christ which will *always* be proclaimed long after this age ends. The gospel of the kingdom is the message with which the Lord will wash His bride in order to cleanse and clothe her in a glorious robe of righteousness. It is also the message that clothes her in military fatigues and army boots to wage spiritual warfare. In fact, all of the other six classes of ministry described here are in reality expressions of the gospel of the kingdom.

3. Prayer and worship.

For meetings to bring life to the body they must be led by the Holy Spirit. The Lord always has a purpose for each gathering. He will have certain things in His heart to express to His children. However, we also have a responsibility. Prayer is *always* the first act of our faith. Time spent in prayer *before* the meeting usually establishes the quality of what takes place. The Spirit's direction for the meeting will become apparent as the saints come into the Lord's presence in worship and praise. As they are free to move spontaneously in spiritual songs behind the leading of minstrels, and as prophetic gifts, exhortations and revelations come forth, a specific theme generally becomes apparent. It is also necessary to know when to be silent while in His presence during worship. The Lord must be worshipped but He *must also be heard!* As we express our love and praise to Him, He will respond to us. In this way His direction is made known.

> ... *When you assemble, EACH one has a psalm, has a teaching, has a revelation, has a tongue, has an interpretation. Let ALL THINGS be done for edification.* (1 Cor. 14:26)

While elders do oversee the meeting, they *must not control* the sequence of events (unless correction is needed). A song leader or meeting director is not the answer. The Lord's desire is to use *many* members in the flow of body ministry. A prophetic spirit resting upon the minstrels is much more important than their musical ability. A good musician without this anointing should sit in the congregation and *follow* the minstrels. The diversity of gifts and ministries of the Spirit that constitute a "good" meeting requires prepared hearts and freedom for spontaneity. Prayer and worship provide the gateway for this to take place.

4. Revelatory Ministry.

As pointed out, prayer and worship in the Spirit open the door for revelatory ministry in a meeting. Revelation may be one or more prophetic messages directed to the congregation as a whole to provide direction for that meeting. However, it may also be a number of messages intended to comfort, exhort or encourage specific individuals. These may be words of knowledge or gifts of prophecy. In such messages, there can be a *predictive* sense to the words. However, *directive* words should only be given to individuals when elders are present (i.e., a presbytery). This ministry is vital in the equipping process for it *confirms* the call and gifting the Lord has placed on individuals. Prophets bear a great responsibility before God to represent Him accurately, not only in the content and timing of their words, but also in their heart attitude when speaking. They should not dilute the impact of the Lord's words by adding their comments, opinion or small talk. They must manifest integrity in *how* they speak as well as in *what* they say.

Since the *only* time directive prophecy may be given is when leaders are present, should other members "hear" such words from the Lord, (and that is possible), their message must be submitted to the leadership. When such guidelines are missing there is great danger of confusion arising from people prophesying over others out of emotions or "wishful thinking." *At all times,* prophecy is to be judged (1 Thess. 5:19-21). Revelatory ministry serves to keep hearts centered on what the Lord is saying at the *present* time. When this ministry is lost, over a period of time hearts of the saints can become dull of hearing. They begin to go their own way emphasizing yesterday's theme. The prophetic eyes of the assembly begins to close, the focus of the church begins to drift into human programs geared to meet needs, and pulpit ministry becomes more given to imparting information (Is. 29:10-13). Elders must always seek for the *now* word of the Lord, and point the people constantly to Him and His purpose as it is unfolded to them. His purpose is centered in building His glorious house.

Revelatory ministry serves to keep our eyes on *Him and the future,* and not on past successes, failures, sins or traditions (Is. 43:18-19; Acts 11:27-28). If a church *only* sees the needs of unsaved mankind, and gives itself solely to winning the lost, it would be like a farmer who harvested his crops without first preparing a barn to store them in. When the vision of a church is centered in the purpose of God, *every ministry* of the body of Christ *can emerge* in time. In the days ahead, many lone-ranger and para-church ministries that were formed to address needs will disappear as the church is restored.

5. Impartation

On occasion the Lord will call, or confirm the call, of a believer to a specific ministry or a new sphere of ministry. This should take place before the local body so that members will know how to pray and support the individual. This ministry should not be entered into hastily or without heart preparation of the candidate and the presbytery. Through prophecy and the anointing of the Holy Spirit, as hands are laid upon the person, there is an impartation of faith to embrace the call. Confirmation should be expected from other prophetic ministries in the body as well as the presbytery (Deut. 34:9; Ro. 1:11; 1 Tim. 1:18; 4:14; Acts 13:1-4).

6. Shepherding.

The pastoral ministries in an eldership undergird and support *all* other ministries by their input to the secular and spiritual spheres of each member's life. Behind their counsel, care, confrontation, family and marriage instruction, and home church guidance lies one underlying goal: to see believers *conformed into the image of Christ!* This is the only standard of righteousness in the church, and it must *never* be diluted or replaced by church laws. Legalism is a great hindrance to true righteousness (Mt. 5:48; Ro. 8:29; 2 Cor. 5:21; Eph. 3:17-19). Character is not developed without pain. Strong winds produce deep roots! Our Father in heaven prunes and disciplines us in love so that we can become partakers of His holiness (Jn. 15:1-17; Heb. 12:5-11). Because His discipline is not pleasant, believers must be equipped to distinguish between attacks of Satan and the hand of God in the circumstances they confront. We are to *always* resist Satan and destroy his works; all believers can do this for greater is He Who indwells us than he who is in the world. At the same time, we are to recognize that when we are *totally* committed to God, *everything* that comes into our lives is there by God's permission. This is true whether it involves overcoming demonic activity or embracing and walking through an unpleasant, difficult circumstance. One produces faith; the other develops character. At such times one has three options: *react to, run from* or *reign over* the circumstance. A vital part of shepherding is assisting saints to make this distinction, and where applicable encouraging them during times of sufferings, trials, persecutions, testings and afflictions for these are what develop character (2 Cor. 4:17; Ro. 5:1-5; 8:17-18; 1 Pet. 1:6-7; 2:21-23; 4:12; 5:6-10; Ja. 1:2-4, 12).

> *And we know that God CAUSES ALL THINGS to work together for good to those who love God, to those WHO ARE CALLED ACCORDING TO HIS PURPOSE.* (Ro. 8:28)

Where verses in the New Testament encourages the reader to endure afflictions, the Greek word, "THLIPSIS" is used which denotes tribulations, such as beatings and imprisonment. Another Greek word, "MASTIX" is also translated as "afflictions" in the gospels (Lk. 7:21; Mk. 3:10). However, when this word is used it always refers to evil spirits and sicknesses which we are to resist.

The following are two other ministry functions related to shepherding. The first is the *very important* service of older women instructing younger women on how to love their husbands and children,and how to relate to their husband in managing home affairs (Tit. 2:3-5). This input is valuable in establishing proper priorities for the husband's ministry. The second ministry function concerns youth meetings, especially those from twelve to around eighteen years of age. There are not two classes of spiritual gifts; one for teenagers and one for adults. Spiritual worship, gifts of the Spirit, along with prayer and intercession, should be a part of youth meetings. Leadership of this meeting should come from a married couple who have both the burden and anointing for it and who are skilled in relating to young people. They are to be encouraged to minister along with the adults in the central meeting.

7. Translocal and apostolic team ministries.

If saints are taught to see only the needs of their local body there exists potential for an elitist spirit to develop in their hearts. This must be avoided; a "we are better than you" attitude is poison in the body of Christ. The saints must not view their local body as an isolated "island of truth", an entity without need of the wider body. A local church is to become self-governing, self-supporting, self-extending but it is *never* self-sufficient! Traveling ministries are vital contributors to the equipping of saints. Visiting ministries, including apostles and prophets, do not function at a governmental level over local elders. They come as bond-servants to minister out of the grace resting upon them in a relationship of trust and accountability with the elders. It is not a matter of simply having one each of the five-fold ministries come and minister and then expect that to be sufficient for all needs. God's anointing and grace will vary even between men with the same call and ministry gift. Each one will be unique in the manner they minister out of their manhood, priesthood and servanthood. *Only* the Lord knows what is needed at any time in an assembly. The elders are responsible to recognize and receive those He sends to them. They are also responsible to judge such ministry.

Just as each local assembly needs the input of trans-local ministries, so also should it in time be equipped to send forth such ministries to plant or water other churches. When ministries are released to travel they are sent as an extension of the local body; the home saints are to view what they do and where they go as something they themselves are a part of. Prayer and financial support are how they demonstrate their involvement.

It is important, therefore, that those sent out return and report what the Lord has accomplished through them. This reinforces the vision of the local church to see the places visited as an extension of themselves, not in an organizational but in a family sense. Thus, assemblies throughout the wider body become relationally and organically bonded together in the life of Christ through translocal ministries.

The value of team ministry to those on the team is *protection* and *accountability;* to those being ministered to it is in the greater richness and *diversity* of what is ministered (2 Cor. 8:16-22; I Cor. 3:6).

One obvious application of team ministry is an apostle and prophet to lay church foundations, however, there are over fifteen teams mentioned in the New Testament; many of which were larger than two and some did not have an apostle.

These teams are ideal vehicles to train young believers with a call to translocal ministry. An example is how Timothy was trained by Paul and other team members.

The ministry of every married man is completed by the gifting of his wife. Her first priority lies in caring for and ministering to their children. When this responsibility does not exist a wife can be a valuable member of her husband's translocal ministry. For example, all the apostles except Paul and Barnabas, took their wives with them on apostolic team ministry (1 Cor. 9:5). Some sisters, apparently single or widows, were also members of Paul's team ministry. Two examples were Phoebe and Priscilla (Ro. 6:1-4). This is in accord with the Lord's promise to anoint both men and women by an outpouring of His Spirit in the last days (Acts 2:18).

Paul did not act as a dictator over the translocal ministries he worked with. For example, he "sent" Timothy (1 Cor. 4:17); he "urged or appealed" to Titus (2 Cor. 8:6, 17); he "asked" Apollos (1 Cor. 16:12) and he called Titus "his partner" (2 Cor. 8:23). In other words, these men sought for accountability, integrity and loyalty in their plurality. It is interesting to note that when Paul writes back to a church they have ministered to, he addresses them as one writing for the team (Gal. 1:1-2; 2 Cor. 1:1; Col. 1:1; Phil. 1:1; 1 and 2 Thess. 1:1).

The Lord's intent in team ministry is greater than simply sending a company of diverse ministries. He selects men who have become strongly bonded in relationship and commitment to each other, who also share a common vision and have ministries that truly complement each other. This appeared to have been the basis of His selection of Paul and Barnabas from among the presbytery at Antioch. It is quite possible that the dissension Paul and Barnabas had over John Mark was an instance when Paul missed God's best (Acts 15:39). Not that Barnabas was right and Paul wrong in their opinions of Mark, but rather that continuing their team ministry should have had first priority in the work God had called them to. One also wonders if Paul would have persisted in his error of going to Jerusalem if Barnabas had been in his team at the time (Acts 21:4,12).

HOME CHURCH MEETINGS

The first requirement for a house church is a Christian home that is in order, where the peace of God rules. Ideally, the husband should be one of the leaders since he is head of the home.

The optimum number for attendance is generally between ten and twenty; once attendance exceeds a range of twenty-five to thirty the family atmosphere becomes more like that of a congregation. When this occurs, there is usually a growing lack of willingness in some to participate in open "give and take", exhortations, praying for one another, sharing scriptures and testimonies. A family atmosphere is reinforced when *all* age levels are present. There should not be home meetings for only one class of believers (i.e. singles, the elderly, etc.).

Home meeting oversight presents an ideal opportunity to equip men for leadership. These would be men who apparently have a call to eldership but are not yet able to meet all the qualifications. Two or more men would serve in this capacity over each home church. Their authority to exercise oversight is delegated by the elders to whom they are accountable. Since they are being trained and tested in their place of oversight they must recognize their service as that of a deacon. *10 Thus, they can be replaced, or asked to lay down their ministry when home or work pressures are too high (1 Tim. 3:10). Also, some may find that they do not have the grace to cope with the responsibility. Experience shows that meeting location and leadership are often subject to change in house churches. The responsibilities of home group leaders is essentially threefold:

1. To care for the saints and oversee meetings.
2. To receive input and counsel from the elders, to work with them and be accountable to them.
3. To function collegially with peers so that a godly mutual dependence builds them together as one person in the eyes of the people. This is an essential part of their training for eldership.

There is no such thing as a *self-made* spiritual leader!

The overall objective for home church meetings can be reduced to one word, *"life."* Leaders are to seek the Lord for guidance on how to motivate the saints toward personal interaction. The first step is to encourage everyone to be relaxed, informal and open to move with the Spirit. An atmosphere of expectancy and spontaneity is required where diverse latent gifts can be discovered and exercised. For this reason, leaders will guard against any one person monopolizing the

* 10: pp 67-73

meeting. They will also prevent cliques from forming. The emphasis is to be *family,* with everyone having opportunity to speak. If irrelevant subjects are introduced the leaders will move with grace to quench them. In all of this, leaders set or maintain direction of the meeting *without controlling it.*

The following ministry activities jointly form a syllabus for equipping the saints:

1. *Prayer and worship*

Ministry to the Lord *always* comes first. One will have little grace in gifts and ministries of the Spirit if he has not first embraced the service of being a priest unto God. One virtue of small groups is that worship in the Spirit is contagious; one or two can affect the others. The elders must ensure there is grace and giftings for worship present in home groups. When good worship and prophetic flow develops in a group, over time the Lord will generally bring forth a diversity of service that is unique for that group. If this flow is not present the group tends to become a carbon copy of some other group. Prayer and worship are *indispensable* for fruitful home church meetings.

2. *Evangelism.*

Every newborn child of God is able to bear effective witness to what the Lord has done in his or her life. Unless witnessing is encouraged immediately after conversion, the burden to do so is often crowded out by subsequent training and teaching. For this reason, evangelism should be given high *priority* in the service of a home church. It should be presented, not as an optional ministry function of the church, but as a life style for every Christian. It is good to set time aside each week to testify of God's grace in the area of outreach. As saints grow in the Lord, and are equipped in new dimensions of character, relationship and ministry they will recognize they are now more capable witnesses for Christ (Mt. 5:13-16; Eph. 5:13-15; 2 Cor. 4:1-2).

> *Conduct yourselves with wisdom toward outsiders, making the most of the opportunity. Let your speech always be with grace, seasoned as it were with salt, so that you may know how you should respond to each person.* (Col. 4:15-16)

When individual believers experience the thrill of seeing souls brought to Christ in group encounters, they will find it much easier to move out in personal evangelism. Thus, it is good for each home church to seek the Lord for direction in how to approach this service. It is easier to just copy what another group is doing, but there is greater virtue in hearing from the Lord for He may lead in a way and to people no one has considered. The following are some evangelistic activities the home groups in the church at Kingston have undertaken:

- Visiting homes for the elderly.
- Drama.
- Visiting public places to witness and hand out tracts.
- Newspaper ads directed to Jehovah Witnesses with personal or recorded messages to those who phone in response to the ads.
- Door-to-door visitation.
- Staffing attractive booths for evangelism at local fairs and business shows.

This subject would not be complete without pointing out the great importance of follow-up ministry for those who make decisions for the Lord.

Finally, home churches should *not* be closed to the unsaved; members should be encouraged to bring unsaved neighbors, strangers, friends or relatives to find the Lord. Those who will be saved provide opportunity for the home group to experience the initial ministries to new converts that are so important, such as water baptism, baptism in the Spirit, etc.

3. *The practice of ministry.*

Physicians practice medicine and Christians practice ministry and neither one becomes perfect at it in this life. The place to practice ministry is not in central meetings, but in home churches. Maturity comes from practice and making mistakes. Each home group is a limited expression of the body of Christ. However, every member in the group has grace of the Spirit with which to bring divine influence into the lives of others. And whether the group is large or small the principle of body ministry is always the same; to exalt and honor the Head by edifying and caring for members of His body.

When there are afflicted and oppressed people present, they should receive first priority in the flow of a meeting.

> *Strengthen hands that are weak and the knees that are feeble and make straight paths for your feet (i.e., set an example) ... SEE TO IT THAT NO ONE COMES SHORT OF THE GRACE OF GOD* ... (Heb. 12:12-13,15)

It is no different than when we hurt some member of our physical body; everything else is set aside until it is ministered to first. Hopefully, prophetic direction for doing so will come from the Lord. If not, the leaders must ask the Lord for wisdom in addressing these needs. One of the elders in Kingston gave the following example of how the Lord led him in such a situation. A very discouraged sister was present. He asked everyone present to silently pray for her and ask the Lord for a word of encouragement to give her. After a period of prayer, they all went to her in turn and gave her their words. the result was a prophetic flow of encouragement that transformed the sister's countenance and spirit.

It can be appropriate for a leader to ask all in the

group to stir up a specific gift of the Spirit and to follow him in ministry. The same approach can be applied to bringing forth spiritual songs of worship. If there arises uncertainty over some issue, it can be instructive to request all members to pray and ask the Lord for a word of knowledge. If the Lord does give a word, its validity will be apparent to the leaders.

Another option is pointing the people to the grace of God by opening the meeting for testimonies of victories that have been recent experiences in lives. Occasionally, it is good to have the people prepare to discuss specific topics that are pertinent to their growth in Christ. The following are suitable examples:

- How our words and attitude affect others.
- What does it mean "to carry our cross"?
- How to face and deal with unpleasant circumstances.
- How to present Christ to family, friends and strangers.
- How to motivate others to commitment.
- How far our submission to one another goes.
- How should we welcome new converts to meetings?
- Specific social issues; how are we to pray, and what are we to do about them?
- Our experiences in the ministry of hospitality.
- How should we respond to cults?
- How to build good relationships in our neighborhoods/at work.
- The disciplines of prayer and Bible study.
- What God's grace has meant to me.
- Personal and family goals in Christ.
- How can we as a group better serve the Lord?
- How can we better serve one another?
- How to improve family devotions.
- How can we serve other local churches, especially denominational assemblies?
- How the Lord taught me to love His people.

Home fellowships provide an excellent place of ministry transition for young people. Teenagers will enter more quickly into worship, sharing, etc., with adults in a small meeting than they would in a large central gathering. Therefore, it is important that they be active in home churches as well as in youth meetings. Because they are the next generation of the Lord's body, leadership should be concerned with helping them make a quick transition to "adult service" in this hour of church restoration.

4. *Building lives together in Christ.*

When believers are linked together by superficial relationships and commitments to one another they will be quickly torn apart in times of trouble and persecution. The great harvest of souls that will be gathered at the close of this present age takes place in times of unprecedented distress, trials, persecution and spiritual warfare. This will require a *strong united* body of believers. Therefore, the Lord is restoring truth on those qualities of the Holy Spirit that bond members together as a functioning body in Christ. Nominal church membership has little or no relevance. Although it is a work of the Holy Spirit we must be yielded, cooperative vessels willing to replace facades with honesty. It is much easier to love those who are honest with you.

Each believer is an individual stone intended for use in the Lord's house. However, in its original state a stone is not yet ready for service. It must first be sanded and shaped to fit the place it is destined for; then it must be cemented (by the love of God) to the stones surrounding it. It is the personal interactions, the "give-and-take" of admonishment and encouragement that sand and shape us to fit together with brothers and sisters.

Iron sharpens iron so one man sharpens another. (Pr. 27:17)

Faithful are the wounds of a friend ... (Pr. 27:6)

Similarly, two members of the Lord's body who work together in service must be united by a healthy "joint" of relationship. Strong "tendons" and "sinews" are needed to hold members in place as they move in unison to serve (Eph. 4:16; Col. 2:19). The stones, joints, tendons and sinews all tell the same story. Our human nature wants to go its own way independent of others; but God says, "learn to love and serve one another, learn to give and receive admonishment in that love; your strength in service lies in being built to your brothers and sisters."

These qualities are not developed in the setting of a traditional meeting. They require more informal times of companionship such as table fellowship, retreats, occasions to share another's joy or sorrow, bearing another's burden, times of giving comfort and encouragement, etc. (Ro. 12:6-18). The Lord will allow needs to develop in certain ones so that as others reach out to help, deeper bonds of compassion and relationship will be built (Eph. 4:28; Titus 3:14; 2 Cor. 1:3-4). Trust and relationship bring a willingness to be more open and honest with others. This vulnerability then becomes a basis for the Lord to adjust certain character traits (Ro. 15:14). Everything spoken in godly admonishment to one who is *not* willing to be open and honest will be interpreted as personal criticism and bear no fruit. These dynamics of relationship, honesty and admonishment are a *continuing process,* for one *cannot trust* the state of his own heart.

For the same reason, the elders also must frequently meet together, not just on church issues, but to be "into" each others lives. Their relationship requires constant attention, for if contentions or stress arises among them it will be felt by the people, even if no details are known. There is *no one* in the family of God who does not have shortcomings in some area of their life. The important thing is to recognize it when others point it out, and then to repent and change. God's word has answers for any personal need or sin. If such things are not dealt with immediately, they become more ingrained in one's character. When this occurs, it becomes vital that repentance and renewal take place, for the individual is now open to demonic activity. If there is no repentance, the issue of character becomes a matter of spiritual warfare. At this time, some of the traits and sins open to demonic oppression are also candidates for spirits of infirmity, both physical and mental.

Table 1 illustrates the progression of many common faults from sin to demonic activity. A major problem is that many simply do not recognize such traits in their lives as sin. This is the reason why we need the input of trusted brothers and sisters into our lives. Discipline is a key word in the process of building character. It can take three forms. First, our heavenly Father prunes us through the discipline of trials and tribulations to redeem faults in our nature that we may not even be aware of (Jn. 15:1-17; Heb. 12:5-11). Second, we exercise self discipline to strengthen areas of our lives we recognize as weak or vulnerable (1 Cor. 9:25-27; 1 Cor. 6:12). Third, one who refuses these first two disciplines, and who continues to sin, can face church discipline (Mt. 18:15-17; Titus 3;10, Ro. 16:17-18). *All* discipline is to be redemptive in purpose: it is never presented as punishment.

Those responsible to equip others should discern such trends in anyone entrusted to their charge. They must also know whether they are dealing with sin in the flesh or demonic activity. The latter can lead to sickness. When this is the case, sickness that is natural (i.e., physical) in cause must not be confused with a spirit of infirmity (Ja. 5:14-16).

TABLE 1 - CHARACTER, SIN AND SPIRITUAL WARFARE

THE PROBLEM SIN	WHEN NOT DEALT WITH	DEMONIC ACTIVITY
Worry	Great Anxiety; Fearful	Dread; Terror; Spirit of Fear
Discouragement	Despair	Hopelessness; Spirit of Suicide
Bad Company and Habits	Pornography	Unclean Spirit; Lust; Perversion
Low Self Worth in Christ	Loner; Withdrawn; Avoids Fellowship	Spirit of Condemnation and Rejection
No Control of Thoughts	Lives a Fantasy	Spirit of Deception; Occult
"Know it All"	Unteachable	Factious, Divisive Spirit
Unfaithful, Undependable	Covenant Breaker	Spirit of Harlotry
No Joy, Always Grieving	Heaviness of Heart	Spirit of Depression
Uncontrolled Anger	Rage	Spirit of Wrath
Desire for Worldly Things	Debt; Poor Stewardship of Money	Spirit of Idolatry; Spirit of Poverty
Dishonest	Hypocrisy	Lying Spirit
Too Self Confident	No Humility or Submission	Spirit of Rebellion
Putting Down Others	Boastful	Spirit of Pride
Unforgiving	Root of Bitterness	Accusing Spirit
Selfish Ambition	Flattery, Manipulative	Controlling Spirit; Jezebel Spirit
Superstitious	Uses Fleeces; Lack of Faith to Hear God	Horoscopes, Occult
Faith Only in Tradition	Legalistic	Religious Spirit
Discontented	Back Biter; Fault Finder	Critical Spirit; Spirit of Hatred
Jealousy, Envy	Gossip	Spirit of Slander
Lack of Prayer	Wrong Priorities	Spirit of Confusion
Faith in Material Things	Greedy	Spirit of Covetousness
Rejects Counsel	Interest in Any New Doctrine	Spirit of Error; Cultic Spirit

By "reading between the lines" one finds an excellent example in the New Testament of a married couple who were well equipped by Paul for their work of service. The couple in question was Aquila and Priscilla. Their history in Scripture covers roughly seventeen years, from AD 53 to AD 67, (the dates are only approximate since Bible scholars do not agree in the dating of epistles). There is no evidence that Aquila was ever considered an elder. Table 2 illustrates their recorded history of service.

TABLE 2 - THE HISTORY OF AQUILA AND PRISCILLA

DATE/SCRIPTURE	**EVENT**
(A.D.53) Acts 18:1-4	Couple arrived from Rome. Worked with Paul as tent maker.
Acts 18:18	Paul took them to Ephesus as pioneers.
Acts 18:24-26	They ministered foundational truth to Apollos, and did so in a hunble way showing the character of Christ
(A.D. 55-56) 1 Cor. 16:19	They now have a church in their home at Ephesus.
Rom. 16:3-5	Back in Rome and have church in their home. Paul implies they have helped all the churches of the Gentiles
(A.D.67) 2 Tim. 4:19	Paul imprisoned; they now are working with Timothy. Apparently back at Ephesus.

A summary of their seventeen year ministry reveals eight *significant* observations that show how well equipped they are.

1. Their secular and spiritual lives were *one*.
2. Husband and wife served together as *one* ministry.
3. They were able to financially support themselves even when they were mobile.
4. They were equipped for translocal team ministry.
5. They were committed to work with and under foundational ministries.
6. They evangelized in the synagogues.
7. Their ministry emphasis was focused on *home churches*.

8. Above all, the record shows that their commitment to Christ included their ministry, their work, their home, as well as their hearts.

May the Lord raise up more couples like Aquila and Priscilla today!

There are two additional benefits of home churches which are not immediately apparent. The first one takes place over time as a local church grows in numbers and introduces home groups in various neighborhoods of its locality. These will spread out geographically as new people come from greater distances. Those groups on the periphery of the area, within which believers attend the church, become candidates for new local assemblies. It may consist of a single home church or be the union of several. In any case, members will already be established in foundational truth, many will be well equipped, they are committed to the local elders, and qualified home group leaders can become elders of the new church. It is a relatively easy task to begin a new local expression of the body of Christ in this manner. The process is similar to mitosis, which is nature's way of multiplying living cells by dividing them. The gospel of the kingdom is likely to have greater impact on an area when there are five churches who work together, each with two hundred members, than it would have if there was one church with a thousand members.

The second advantage is one I refer to as "hidden leaders." A book was recently written by a well-known Christian leader who visited China to discover the status of Christians in that land. [17] He was astonished at the number and quality of underground churches that met only in homes. He pointed out that when sudden cataclysmic persecution came from the communists, their first act was to kill or imprison the leaders. This was catastrophic to the nominal traditional churches. Leaders had to compromise or be removed. In the typical centralized church structure there is no one to take their place, and without leadership the church ceases to be effective.

However, in the decentralized structure, where there is no clergy-laity distinction, and where each member is being equipped to serve; should persecution come and elders are taken away, the "hidden leaders" of home churches become the new elders. Meetings would remain confined to homes, but there would be little impact on the effectiveness of ministry.

Home churches play a vital role in the Lord's plan to equip the saints and restore His church.

CONCLUSION

It is very important that those who know and love the Lord Jesus keep their eyes focused on Him as He builds and prepares the church for His return. We are to be a people whose hearts thrill with expectancy for the future, not clouded with visions of the past.

> *Behold, the former things have come to pass, now I declare new things; before they spring forth I proclaim them to you.* (Is. 42:9)

> *Do not call to mind the former things, or ponder things of the past. Behold, I will do something new, now it will spring forth; will you not be aware of it?* .... (Is. 43:18-19)

> ... *I proclaim to you new things from this time, even hidden things which you have not known.* (Is. 48:6)

> ... *I press on in order that I may lay hold of that for which also I was laid hold of by Christ Jesus. Brethern, I do not regard my self as having laid hold of it yet; but one thing I do: forgetting what*

> *lies behind and reaching forward to what lies ahead, I press on toward the goal for the prize of the upward call in Christ Jesus.* (Phil. 3:12-14)

It is a time of new beginnings; there is a new awareness of the days in which we live, a new reality in challenges, transitions and dimensions of ministry. It is a time when the Lord will execute His word upon the earth thoroughly and quickly. All that has been built in the church by the strength and imaginations of man will be shaken and fall; *only* what has been built on the Lord will stand!

Daniel prophesied that knowledge would increase in the last days (Dan. 12:4). How true this is turning out to be! Total knowledge doubles in an ever decreasing amount of time, primarily through discoveries in the various disciplines of science We are truly living in the age of information! Advances in computer science has now opened the door to artificial intelligence; who knows where that will lead?

These advances in science will become significant modifiers of social, military and economic strategies in the days ahead. To some, they will promote a false assurance that man can come up with answers for his problems; this, of course, is not the case. However, to the church, they represent technologies that the Lord will use to help reach all mankind with the gospel. The reformation began by using technology from the Renaissance, primarily the printing press. The final period of restoration will close using technologies of the information age.

Unprecedented days of turmoil and change lie ahead. Deep darkness and deception is coming upon the world. However, it will be also a time of the *greatest demonstration* of the gospel of the kingdom ever witnessed by mankind. The body of Christ is being prepared as an ark of safety for all whose hearts will turn to the Lord. New dimensions of power and unity will be manifest by God's people and be used to bring thousands upon thousands from the nations into the church. A transcendent glory will rest upon the church. In that day the Lord *alone* will be exalted as members of His body lose their identity in Him.

> *Arise, shine; for your light has come, and the GLORY of the Lord has risen upon you. For behold, DARKNESS will cover the earth, and DEEP DARKNESS the peoples; but the Lord will arise upon you, and HIS GLORY WILL APPEAR UPON YOU. And nations will come to your light, and kings to the brightness of your rising. Lift up your eyes round about, and see; THEY ALL GATHER TOGETHER, THEY COME TO YOU. Your sons will come from afar, and your daughters will be carried in the arms* (Is. 60:1-4).

We are living in crucial days of *restoration* and *transition.* Significant *changes* must be made by many if they are to be participants and not just spectators of these events. The infrastructure of church bodies must be prepared to accommodate great numbers of new converts, many with severe problems. Because of shortages that will arise in natural means of supply, new dimensions of faith will be required by the church to meet the needs of those who turn to Christ. The Lord Himself will be that supply through the creative word of faith. The Lord has restored the pattern for building local expressions of His body in order that the saints might be equipped for the great work that will close this age. However, the harvest is *so immense* that the *whole* body of Christ must work as *one* under the leadership of the Holy Spirit. Differences in such things as church government, doctrinal emphasis, etc., *must not* hinder the unity that will be necessary for this great work to take place. Leaders must not judge and tear down methods or ministries of other Christian bodies; they are to reach out as *servants* to help and seek to be allies in the fields of harvest. Above all, they are to give themselves as men of truth to equip those saints entrusted to them for their work of service and for their place in the glory to come.

APPENDIX: THE NEW AGE MOVEMENT

PREFACE

Each person has access to two doors in his life — one is the door of the heart, which can only be opened by a latch on the inside. The Lord Jesus knocks on this door for us to invite Him in.

The other door also can only be opened by a latch on our side. It is the door of our mind. Satan knocks on this door to entice us to open and receive psychic knowledge of the occult world.

The door of one's heart is the way into the kingdom of God; if our heart is closed to the Lord, then our mind can become a way of deception into a kingdom of darkness and death. The knocker Satan is using today on the other side of this door is the New Age message.

> *There is a way which seems right to a man, but its end is the way of death.* (Prov. 14:12)

His strategic emphasis is not what we might believe it to be. It is not atheism or communism that will deceive most of mankind. On the contrary, Satan is emphasizing the spiritual realm. His current word to the world is "be spiritual; understand the mysteries that will unlock your full potential. You are God."

Man was created for God, Who placed within each of us a desire that can only be satisfied when we come to know Him. Thus, in human nature there is an inner hunger to explore the mysteries of the spirit world. The issue is whether we will meet God's conditions for coming to know Him as expressed in the gospel, or will be drawn away by carnal desires to explore the psychic world of the occult. Do we heed the gentle voice of the Holy Spirit to our hearts, or the call of Satan to self-exaltation? The issue is one of life or death!

THE MYSTERY OF GODLINESS

The Christian faith is based on God's mystery, which is Christ Himself (Col. 2:2-3). Jesus came to earth as God in the flesh, where He lived a perfect and sinless life. This incarnation of God is a mystery. Then, out of love for us, He willingly took all of mankind's sin upon Himself and became sin on our behalf. Bearing our sin, He died in our place on the cross. Because He was innocent, He became our sin offering and was resurrected from the dead. Being glorified, He was then raised up and seated at the right hand of the Father where He now intercedes for us. These truths are spoken of in scripture as a mystery (1 Tim. 3:16).

Whenever a person believes in Him as He is revealed in the gospel, repents of his sin and personally accepts the Lord Jesus as Savior, his sins are forgiven and Christ comes to indwell that person, to live in him and bring forth righteousness. This indwelling presence of God in man is also described in Scripture as a great mystery (Col. 1:25-27).

Salvation and the way of godliness are mysteries because they are *only* understood and possessed through *revelation* to our hearts. They do not come via reasoning or intellect. We can only be saved through faith in Him who is *revealed* to our *hearts* by the Holy Spirit.

> *... if you confess with your mouth Jesus as Lord, and believe* ***in your heart*** *that God raised Him from the dead, you shall be saved; for* ***with the heart man believes****, resulting in righteousness, and with the mouth he confesses, resulting in salvation.* (Rom. 10:9-10)

Salvation is based on *regenerated hearts;* not on enlightened minds! This absolutely *vital distinction* must be clearly proclaimed in the gospel we preach, for the world today faces the greatest mental deception with which Satan has ever tempted mankind! The climax of his delusion will be the mystery of lawlessness, which is Satan's final step in his strategy of rebellion against God.

THE MYSTERY OF LAWLESSNESS

The final conflict of the ages for the souls of men is even now beginning. I believe every person will be brought to a place of decision for or against the Lord before Jesus returns. The gospel of the kingdom shall be preached in the whole world for a witness to all nations; as a result, a great harvest will be gathered in the church as thousands upon thousands are converted to Christ.

Although multitudes are redeemed, there will also be a falling away of many. These, not being established in the faith, will be drawn into the occult by Satan's deception.

> *But the Spirit explicitly says that in later times some will fall away from the faith, paying attention to* ***deceitful spirits*** *and* ***doctrines*** *of* ***demons.*** (1 Tim. 4:1)
>
> *And at that time* ***many*** *will fall away and will deliver up one another and hate one another. And* ***many*** *false prophets will arise and mislead* ***many****. And because lawlessness is increased, most people's love will grow cold.* (Matt. 24:10-12)

Those who will not receive the love of the truth so as to be saved will be deceived into believing what is false. The apex of this deception concerns what scripture calls the "man of lawlessness" (or the antichrist), a man of sin who will ultimately be indwelt by Satan (2 Thess. 2:3-12). He will be incarnate, having a bodily form and substance.

The deception that will lead people to believe this man is based on mighty demonstrations of occultic power, lying signs and false wonders. These activities will take place over a period of time under an umbrella of a mind-oriented "theology" known as the New Age Movement. Although it is in reality the doctrine of demons, New Age teaching has been fashioned so as to have mental appeal to peoples of both Eastern and Western cultures.

The man of sin will emerge as the dominant authority figure and leader in world affairs. He will appear to have answers for monumental problems concerning military, economic, religious and political issues that face the nations. He will proclaim a new age of enlightenment, the Astrological New Age of Aquarius in which there will be one world government and one world religion.

The mystery of lawlessness will eventually be recognized by the world for who he is — to their sorrow when they understand that Satan has become incarnate in him. Satan will enter this man so that he will be worshiped as God by the world, for this he has desired above all else from the beginning!

During this terrible period of trouble, the antichrist will control commerce and permit no one to buy or sell without taking his mark (the mark of the beast) upon either their right hand or their forehead. It will apparently involve a luciferian rite; in any case, to take his mark is to be *eternally lost* (Rev. 13:16-17; 14:11; 16:2; 19:20). This time of testing will be brought to an end by the coming of the Lord.

In order to avoid these snares of the devil and to be able to clearly and intelligently warn others, one must be able to recognize New Age activities and teaching in the light of God's Word. This is necessary if the church is to be effective in evangelizing those who are candidates for this deception. Christians have *nothing* to fear from Satan. We are to overcome him and expose his works. The tools we have been given to accomplish this are the gospel in its simplicity and the gifts and ministries of the Holy Spirit (James 4:7-8; Eph. 6:10-18).

THE NEW AGE MOVEMENT

(1) ORIGIN

Practices and teachings of the New Age are not new; they have been around for centuries! In the 1960's, evil spirits from the East began to have a growing influence upon nations of the West. This came about through an influx of swamis and gurus from India, and because of the many in the drug scene who went to India to consult such people. It is significant to note that this took place during the charismatic renewal; it was apparently Satan's reaction to a work of the Holy Spirit.

In 1975, various groups involved in the occult came

together to form the "New Age Movement." It is a growing entity that is best described as a loosely-linked communication network of diverse psychic/occultic literature and teaching in which there is mutual support but no one overall leader. [18,19,20]

It represents an umbrella of "theology" that unites common occultic themes and practices, even bringing together groups with quite different emphases, such as witchcraft and astrology. Together they are like a mighty octopus with tentacles of deceit and death reaching out to every section of society. This is the deep darkness that the prophet Isaiah saw covering the earth in the last days (Is. 60:2).

(2) WHAT IS ITS MESSAGE?

The New Age movement promises a counterfeit millennium, the astrological New Age of Aquarius. This is to be an age of enlightenment without the God of the Bible, where man is enthroned. The concepts of God, the world, man and salvation are taken from classic Hinduism, as are many related mystical experiences. It is pantheistic in that God and nature are one. There is one ultimate kind of matter for all things. If all is one, then there can be no sin, death or guilt of sin. Therefore, the substitutionary death of Christ is meaningless. Hinduism agrees that Jesus is God, but no more than we can be. He simply achieved "Christ consciousness," something we can all attain. Apart from this life, one can also reach higher levels of existence through cycles of reincarnation.

The pantheistic God is impersonal, neither speaking nor acting. Space and time are considered illusions. Thus, there is no concept of divine revelation as in Christianity. Rather, spiritual knowledge is always available to anyone who, by an "altered state of consciousness," is able to perceive it. This is where demonic deception comes into play. The mental ability to penetrate the illusion of space and time, and thereby achieve this new state of consciousness, comes from mystical occultic experiences. For example, through medium contact, guidance in the form of messages is received from spirit beings who falsely identify themselves as "extra terrestials from other galaxies," or as persons who have lived on earth at some time in the past. However, they are demons whose objective is to deceive and entrap the listener.

The pyschic messages given to the inquirers are oriented toward the *mind* and *ego*, designed to turn the listener to himself and away from God and His word. They contradict what scripture teaches on repentance, the need for forgiveness of sin, God's judgment, the blood of Christ, the nature and person of God, etc. The following are some examples of messages that have been received:

- "Love yourself; you are God."
- "You have lived before."
- "There are many paths to God; choose your own."
- "There is no eternal Savior, no atonement for sin, no hell, no resurrection, no judgment."
- "All religions are one."
- "The New Age God exists as energy that is vibrating everywhere in the universe; get into harmony with it and achieve higher planes of awareness."
- "Suffering, heartbreak, sickness and death are all opportunities to wake up; especially death. All is good."
- "There is no good or evil; both are two sides of the same coin."
- "The belief that you are bad, a form of evil, distorts your vision and self-esteem. This belief enables you to produce negative results in the world. You are made of the same stuff God is and that is nothing but God. You are good. You are not evil. No one is evil."

One does not have to go to a medium for messages that have a common theme with these. Psychotherapists who teach a selfist psychology emphasizing self-love, self-seeking, self-esteem and self-actualization present a mental foundation upon which New Age deception can be built. Two such well-recognized programs are E.S.T. [Erhard Seminars Training] and Silva Mind Control. These are a blend of human potential psychology and Eastern mysticism. Striving to raise one's human potential through love of self by self-assertion and self-confidence can lead to self-deification. It is wise to remember that pride is the father of all sin, and that humility is the mark of greatness in God's kingdom.

The Bible teaches us to exercise self-control and self-discipline, and to measure our individual worth in terms of how much God loves us, recognizing the price He paid for our salvation.

(3) THE SUBTLE APPEAL OF THE NEW AGE

The message of classic Hinduism would not appeal to a typical Western mind. It teaches that what is earthly is in direct conflict with the spiritual. Therefore, anyone seriously seeking salvation should renounce the world and its pleasures. The world and events in it are an illusion and therefore obstacles to overcome. This emphasis can be seen in the so-called Hindu "holy men," who go about naked, without possessions and often covered with ashes.

To appeal to Western culture, the New Age movement has modified this aspect of Hinduism to now affirm the value of world realities such as people, culture, peace, the environment, education, politics, etc. Instead of "turn on, tune in and drop out," as Timothy Leary used to preach during the 1960's in his endorsement of Hinduism, candidates today are offered the challenge of changing the world by preparing for the New Age of enlightenment. For example, groups of New Agers will come together for collective meditation and to harmonize their psychic energy in an attempt to bring peace or for some other "good cause."

They also place much emphasis on improving one's self and one's work capability with psychological self-esteem teaching. The blend of self-actualization with psychic phenomena, along with a challenge to change the world, is what makes the New Age movement so subtle and appealing to the uninformed.

Western culture has been prepared for the New Age movement by the teachings of various Mind Science cults (e.g. Theosophy; Christian Science; Unity). The theology of these groups was a 19th century occultism mixed with certain Hindu concepts.

The teaching of evolution has helped prepare the way for the New Age concept of cosmic evolution, where one supposedly evolves into a higher plane of existence through cycles of reincarnation. In a similar sense, secular humanism is a stepping-stone to self-deification.

It is easy to understand how these ungodly teachings can appeal to the unregenerated man.

(4) NEW AGE STRATEGY

There are *two* primary objectives that comprise the New Age strategy to change the world.

(i) Personal Transformation

This is a psychic counterfeit of Christian regeneration. Individuals are "transformed" when they achieve an altered (higher) consciousness. New Agers also speak of this experience as a "paradigm shift" (a shift in one's perspective of reality). However, Christians recognize the experience as being demonized. This unfortunate state usually begins by what appears to be an innocent, harmless experiment or technique that promises to increase one's potential. It may also start as an exercise to satisfy one's curiosity about magic or the unknown. The critical step is to seek guidance in personal decisions from the psychic realm rather than from God.

This state is arrived at through one or more mystical/ psychic experiments in which contact is made with the spirit world. When a medium is used (often while in a trance), as in a seance, the spirit contacted will generally pretend to be someone known to the inquirer, a friend or relative who has died. Familiarity with personal details are used to deceive the listener. A channel is a medium who supposedly can contact an entity who died thousands of years ago and has now "evolved" to the state of "ancient masters," "ascended masters," "masters of wisdom" or "wise ones." Other names given by "less exalted" spirits are "light bearers," "spirit guides," "inner guides," "imaginary guides," "inner teachers," etc. In *all* cases, the messages are from demons who the Bible calls "familiar spirits."

There are other practices that the New Age encourages to lead one into contact with the spirit world apart from any medium. Three of the most significant are the use of psychedelic drugs, obsession with hard (metallic) rock music and fantasy role-playing games, such as "Dungeons and Dragons."

(ii) Planetary Transformation

The New Age movement seeks to win sufficient individuals so as to be able to change the world. To accomplish this, they focus on leaders and persons of social influence in the professions, especially education, the media, politics, religion, health care and psychology. Education appears to have been given highest priority. Their influence in our schools is significant and increasing.

(5) NEW AGE PRACTICES AND PSYCHOTECHNIQUES

The following are some occultic practices plus supporting psychological beliefs and experiences that abound in the New Age movement. These are all demonic in origin and are to be avoided by Christians.

- Astrology (use of horoscopes and astrological charts to make decisions)
- Crystals (wearing crystals to ward off negative forces; gazing into crystal balls for fortune telling)
- Spiritualist churches; Religious science; etc.
- Tarot cards (used along with astrology and numerology in divination)
- Ouija boards
- Pendulum prophecy (divination by pendulum motion)
- Seances and channeling (medium contact with the spirit world)
- Yoga
- Transcendental Meditation (T.M.)
- U.F.O. experiences/encounters
- Witchcraft
- Reincarnation
- Clairvoyance (power to perceive matters beyond human ability)
- ESP
- Precognition (predicting future events)
- Telepathy (transfer of one's thoughts to another's mind)
- Out of body experiences
- Mind Control Therapy (e.g., e.s.t., Silva Mind Control, etc.)
- Self-induced Creative Visualization (i.e., psychologically-initiated visions)
- Satanism (most New Agers would not knowingly worship Satan)

The word of God *clearly warns us not to* practice such things.

> *Do not turn to mediums or spiritists; do not seek them or be defiled by them. I am the Lord your God.* (Lev. 19:31)
>
> *As to the person who turns to mediums and to spiritists, to play the harlot after them, I will set My face against that person and will cut him off from among his people.* (Lev. 20:6)
>
> *There shall not be found among you anyone ... who uses divination, one who practices witchcraft, or one who interprets omens or a sorcerer, or one that casts a spell, or a medium, or a spiritist, or one who calls up the dead. For whoever does these things is detestable to the Lord....* (Deut. 18:10-12)
>
> *But the ... unbelieving ... the murderers, immoral persons and* ***sorcerers*** *... their part will be in the lake that burns with fire and brimstone which is the second death.* (Rev. 21:8)

THE CHURCH AND THE NEW AGE

Satan has three approaches to draw persons into error and deception. To one who has limited understanding of God's ways, he will present error as truth and darkness as light. To one with greater understanding and spiritual awareness of God's word, he brings a mixture of truth and error. To one who is Spirit-filled and committed to walking in the light of all revealed truth, he brings an over-emphasis of some truth to the extent that there is an unbalance in the message preached, which can lead to error. In all cases, he seeks to instill pride and self-sufficiency in the people who will listen to him. To have spiritual pride in one's heart is to shake hands with the devil!

There are significant numbers of people in or on the periphery of traditional mainline churches who are potential candidates for New Age deception. Any demonstration of supernatural power can appear to them to be a work of God. The New Age attempts to infiltrate such churches. New Agers will speak with glowing enthusiasm about God (to them, a cosmic force or energy) and about atonement (to them, at-one-ment with nature and the universe). The New Age "gospel" they preach is presented as an extension of the gospel of the Bible. They will speak of the new birth (meaning reincarnation) and the goodness of religion (referring to all religions). They will promote psychotherapy techniques as the way to attain greater spirituality (such as yoga, T.M., mind control, etc.). In all of these endeavors, they will frequently quote scripture, but always out of context and never so as to encourage a study of the Bible.

Fundamental Christians with a strong emphasis on knowing scripture, but who are not Spirit-filled and are therefore unfamiliar with spiritual gifts, would not normally be attracted to psychic experiences in the occult. In fact, out of fear of all supernatural manifestations they draw back from being equipped with true spiritual gifts. As a consequence, they are weakened in their ability to help deliver those in bondage or demonized from the occult. In addition, because their emphasis is oriented more towards the mind and knowledge, they can be susceptible to subtle mental avenues of deception. The most obvious example is the use of "Christian" psychology for counseling rather than simply using the word of God. Psychology and the message of self-worth and self-actualization in dealing with the psyche and mind of those with personal problems easily leads into the psychotherapy practices of the New Age movement.

Another example can be found in certain holistic health teachings that have been adopted from Eastern religions. These appeal to the mind while appearing to offer hope to those who are ill. The refined foods, chemical additives and junk foods of our culture also encourage this trend. However, New Agers believe that health is a matter of energy, not material matter. They teach that our body is affected by cosmic forces of energy, and that one can manipulate this spiritual energy to gain health. This is accomplished through certain relaxation exercises (e.g., yoga), meditation and diet (e.g., vegetarianism, etc.). The body is considered an instrument, along with the mind, in the quest for self-deification. It must be carefully tuned for harmony with the universal energy. Some words used to speak of this body-energy relationship include prana, ch'i, ying and yang. This is clearly another door that can lead into occult experiences and practices. One of the doctrines of demons prophesied for the last days is "to abstain from certain foods" (1 Tim. 4:3).

A Spirit-filled Christian is not immune from the forces of deception. Truth emphasized to the extreme becomes error. We cannot over-emphasize any one truth without beginning to neglect another. The fault for such an unbalance usually can be traced to placing too much emphasis on one's ability to understand, on knowledge and reasoning, and not depending enough on the Lord and power of the Holy Spirit.

One example is an over-emphasis on seeking spiritual guidance through what is called visualization, where a believer searches in a disciplined fashion with his imagination for an image of the Lord. The image will then "come to life" in his imagination and converse with the seeker, who keeps a journal record of the conversation. The New Age adherents teach that we can bring into existence whatever we visualize, since "we create our own reality." Thus, one can tap into an unlimited potential by visualizing whatever he wishes, such as wealth and possessions for himself. The question one must ask is whether such an image is a "mental idol" or a reality of the Lord Himself.

Much of the psychology used to support used to support visualization came from the work of Carl Jung, a world famous psychologist who developed his teaching through messages from a psychic (demonic) guide. Jung was a demonized occultist for most of his life, and the revelations and visions he received from the spirit world was the basis of his teaching.

The Lord has made provision for all the spiritual guidance we will ever need. He has given His word for instruction, and He gives us the Holy Spirit to reveal Himself and His word to us. He has also given certain gifts of the Holy Spirit that specifically bring truth to us. These include the word of knowledge, the word of wisdom, the discerning of spirits and the three prophetic gifts. In addition, if He wishes to reveal something new to us He can do so by visions or if we are asleep, by dreams. Both dreams and visions are initiated by the Lord. He also speaks into our hearts as we seek Him in prayer and worship. It is by these avenues that we can have the mind of Christ; and in *all* cases the Lord brings truth to us through our *spirit*. Our interface to God is by our *heart* and *not* by our *mind* or imagination! There is no "latent" or undeveloped power in the human mind; power comes from the spirit realm, either from the Lord or from demons.

Revelation is a God-initiated anointing of our spirit, visualization is a psychologically-initiated exercise of the imagination that can lead to idols of the mind. The Spirit of God enlightens the eyes of our hearts (Eph. 1:18); the New Age seeks to enlighten the mind. Imagination is not reality!

Normal visualization can be good and motivational, but not when taken to an extreme by attempting to manipulate God. It is equally wrong to allow one's imagination to run wild in fantasies, or to visualize money and possessions one may want, believing that it is possible to materialize them through the power of one's imagination. The occult can do such things through demonic power, even to the extent of bending metal and producing levitation.

The issue is the role and nature of the mind. The original fall came through Satan's temptation of Eve in this area. Because a weakness in our minds has been inherited from our first parents, the Bible instructs us to renew and control our minds (Rom. 12:1-3; 2 Cor. 10:5). Renewal begins with the new birth as we humble ourselves in repentance, confess our sins, and as a little child believe His word and accept Him as our Savior. However, the renewal process continues as we grow in Christ. We must always guard our thought life and imagination, for the way of maturity is not the way of self-exaltation; it is the lowly way that Jesus taught us to learn from Him (Matt. 11:29; 5:3-12). The emphasis is never on ourselves; it is always on Him. Who *He is in us* is far more important than who *we are in Him*. Both are true, but the emphasis must be on Him!

> *But I am afraid, lest as the serpent* ***deceived*** *Eve by his craftiness,* ***your mind*** *should be led astray from the* ***simplicity*** *and purity of devotion to Christ.* (2 Cor. 11:3)

The gospel is the power of God for salvation to everyone who believes (Rom. 1:16). The simplicity of the gospel is the answer to all who seek life and reality. It is out of the simplicity of our mind and the hunger of our heart that we can know the mysteries of God.

Jesus asks everyone who is in bondage to sin, the poor, the oppressed, the hurting and the unloved, to come to Him. He loves you and will save you.

If you are one who is involved in the occult, and you want to be free and become a child of God, you *must* renounce Satan and forsake the occult as you repent and pray to receive the Lord into your heart.

[Much of this material was taken from a course taught on the New Age movement by Ah-Tua-Teo and Peter Rogati of Catskill, New York, to whom I extend my thanks.]

BIBLIOGRAPHY

1. David Webber, PROPHETIC PROSPECTS FOR ISRAEL; The Gospel Truth Publication, P.O. Box 1144, Oklahoma City, OK 73101; Jan. 1988.

2. Arthur Wallis, THE RADICAL CHRISTIAN; (revised), Cityhill Publishing, 4600 Fellowship Road, Columbia, MO 65203; 1987.

3. Richard M. Riss, LATTER RAIN; Kingdom Flagship Foundation, P.O. Box 160, Etobicoke, Ontario, Canada M9C4V2; 1987.

4. John W. Kennedy, THE TORCH OF THE TESTIMONY; Christian Books, Galeta, California; 1965.

5. J. B. Lightfoot, THE APOSTOLIC FATHERS; Baker Book House, Grand Rapids, Michigan; 1987.

6. Dr. Bill Hamon, THE ETERNAL CHURCH; Christian Int. Publishers, Point Washington, Rt. 2, Box 351, Florida; 1982.

7. E. H. Broadbent, THE PILGRIM CHURCH; Zondervan Publishers, 1415 Lake Drive, S.E. Grand Rapids, Michigan 49506; 1985.

8. Philip Schaff, HISTORY OF THE CHRISTIAN CHURCH: Vol. 1; Charles Scribner, New York, N.Y., 1882.

9. L. P. Qualben, A HISTORY OF THE CHRISTIAN CHURCH: Thomas Nelson & Sons, New York, NY; 1933.

10. Dale Rumble, THE DIAKONATE; Destiny Image, P.O. Box 351, Shippensburg, PA; 17257; 1982.

11. Dale Rumble, PREPARED FOR HIS GLORY; Destiny Image, P.O. Box 351, Shippensburg, PA; 17257; 1986.

12. Dr. Bill Hamon, PROPHETS AND PERSONAL PROPHECY; Destiny Image Publishers, P.O. Box 351, Shippensburg, PA; 17257; 1988.

13. J.B. Lightfoot, THE CHRISTIAN MINISTRY; Edited by Dr. Philip E. Hughes; Morehouse-Barlow, 78 Danbury Road, Wilton, Conn. 06897; 1987.

14. George Eldon Ladd, THE LAST THINGS; William B. Eerdsmans Publishing Co., 255 Jefferson Ave., S.E., Grand Rapids, Mich. 49503; 1978.

15. Donald Rumble, WINDS OF CHANGE; Destiny Image, P.O. Box 351, Shippensburg, PA 17257; 1987.

16. Trevor Dearing, SUPERNATURAL SUPERPOWERS; Logos International, Plainfield, New Jersey; 1977.

17. Arthur Wallis, CHINA MIRACLE; Cityhill Publishing, 4600 Christian Fellowship Road, Columbia, MO, 65203; 1986.

18. Douglas Groothuis, CONFRONTING THE NEW AGE; Intervarsity Press; 1988.

19. Douglas Groothuis, UNMASKING THE NEW AGE; Intervarsity Press; 1986.

20. Karen Hoyt, THE NEW AGE RAGE; Revell; 1987.